ECO CIVILIZATION 2140

A Twenty-Second-Century History and Survivor's Journal

Roy Morrison

Printed in the United States

ISBN #: 1-930149-37-9

Library of Congress Number applied for.

Writer's Publishing Cooperative
P.O. Box 201
Warner, NH 03278
rmjsc@mcttelecom.com

Orders:
Trade: Ingram (under Enfield Distribution)
Individuals and Institutions: Enfield Distribution 1-888-874-6904
On line: Amazon.com

Website: www.essentialbooks.com

Book design by Barbara Jones, Lebanon N.H.
Cover art (Hasten Slowly) by Josh Yunger

ECO CIVILIZATION 2140

A Twenty-Second-Century History and Survivor's Journal

Dedication:

To Samuel Schaffer-Morrison

and to

My Sisters and Brothers of the of the Clamshell Alliance and our Nonviolent Struggles Past, Present, and Future.

Contents

Author's Note in a Bottle

An author unbearded, without pseudonym or ghost, is in the position of a new parent.

I did it. I admit it.

But certainly I had help that includes the indispensable assistance of friends and the kindness of strangers. And the backstory, beyond the obvious, is carried in our culture and our genes and leads back beyond Hebrews and Helenizers ultimately to the contributions of that first quickening perhaps in a tidal pool along a Pangean coast billions of years past.

The second question: Why'd you do it, is more interesting. It challenges me to come clean—be a standup guy and confess in this age where explanation is become part of a choreographed ritual of admission. This also offers me the opportunity to trade the tiresome deconstructionist claim of a limitless trove of valid meanings for a nod toward personal agency and free will in a self-conscious universe.

So, for me . . .

Eco Civilization 2140 reverses the telescope, looking backward on an ecological civilization after the fact. While yet another distopian vision of things to come would take almost no one's breath away. *Eco Civilization 2140* posits quite a different denoument for our current struggles.

Democracy, freedom and community shall have their way. Our future to come, albeit after much effort and trouble, will be free, prosperous, and pleasurable. By the middle of the 22nd century an ecological civilization will have emerged from our unsustainable industrial present.

In my personal journey, on reflection, this prospect and possibility began to take shape during my time as a member of the South Friendly Cluster of the Clamshell Alliance, 220 of us, camped out on Tony and Maria Santasucci's land bordering the Seabrook nuclear power plant construction site in New Hampshire in April 1977.

After much discussion and deliberation, we left the sheltering woods and climbed single file with our backpacks up and over that high construction rock pile under the yes and helicopters of the N.H. State Police. We faced our fears. We occupied the Seabrook site and built a transient and yet miraculous community. And then many of us spent almost two weeks incarcerated in a NH national Guard Armory.

It was from this experience that the molecules of social change were shaken most vigorously and put into motion with new possibilities of self-management, non-violence, democracy, creativity, freedom and community, and love emergent and manifest. Healing change is not just a distant possibility. It is part of who we are and what we can do.

Eco Civilization 2140 is one vision of what is emerging from the troubles and opportunities of our industrial civilization. It's offered as much as provocation as prediction. It's meant to be a tool to assist you along the path.

At Seabrook in 1977 some of us brought shovels, unbidden even by our *Occupier's Handbook*, shovels that helped us construct the lineaments of an unplanned but self-organizing and quickly evolving and glorious encampment.

Don't underestimate the power of a tool or of an idea.

Enjoy.

Roy Morrison
Back House Studio
Warner, NH

November 27, 2005

Foreword

Writers, like farmers, are stubborn folk, refusing to give in to calamitous circumstances, insisting in the belief that they can bring into being a more fruitful reality. The pedagogical foundation to the writing endeavor has fallen into disrepute in our postmodern era, but our best writers still respond creatively to the dire necessity surrounding us in the form of oppressive economic and governmental institutions, a growing litany of environmental catastrophe which threatens earthly creation, a rising tide of poverty and migrations of refugees, to imagine better, more perfect conditions.

Roy Morrison has followed in this utopian and missionary tradition, bringing us the seeds, a vision of where we can go from here. In this book, Morrison has affirmed the possibility of a human centered and locally based development, providing an antiterrorist balm to our fractured, despairing and colonized collective mind. A primer for activists as much as a futuristic tale of a beneficent, sane, sustainable rural New England for literary appetites, *Eco Civilization 2140: A Twenty-Second-Century History and Survivor's Journal* is a blueprint for all who share in the work of imagining a better place for the human family to flourish.

Anthony Caplan
Mink Hills Center for
Sustainable Development
Henniker, New Hampshire

Chronology of Events Great and Small

1950-2100	The Age of Pollution
1950s	Happy Days of industrialism
2000-2030	The Empire of Oil. Resource wars
2009 & 2014	Oil reaches Hulbert Peak with half global resources consumed, and production irrevocably declines
	"The Double Steals": Warner's Mark Govoni playing for the Marlins, steals home against the Red Sox in seventh and ninth inning of World Series, seventh game
2015	Newton-Ladd orchard in Warner pioneers organic fruit growing techniques
2030-2050	Dramatic global warming
2030-2040	Bailouts of oil and banking industries and recession
2040-2060	The Great Crisis: pandemics, war, and ecological crisis
2047	New Hampshire and Vermont town meetings pass warrants calling for an end to resource wars and a charter for ecological sustainability
2048	Global population peaks at nine billion
2052	The Great Panic: financial institutions collapse
2054	Invention of catalysts for solar electrolysis of water
2070	Climate begins to stabilize
2070-2090	"The East Is Green." China leads the way to ward sustainability
2073	Warner Town Meeting votes for community entrepreneurship and community cooperatives
2074	Global WMD Treaty bans all weapons of mass destruction
2075-2100	The Great Political Reawakening
2076	Ecological taxes on pollution, depletion, and ecological damage and an end to all income taxes
2077	Negative income tax to end poverty as a citizenship right for all who perform national service
2078	American Trust for investment in sustainability
2079	American Trust bonds
	Mag-lev system between New Hampshire and Boston
2085	Joint master's degrees offered at Harvard from Divinity and Business Schools
2091	American Union formed from Arctic to Tierra del Fuego
2094	Northern New England Republic and Southern New England

	Confederacy organized
2095	Universal Declaration of Human Rights and Sustainability
2100	The Age of Contentment begins
2101	First Global Bowl played
2102	Warner Nanotech Enterprises organized; farmers grow organic feedstocks from yellow mustard and cannabis
2103	The Happiness Index (HI) replaces GDP as economic measure
2104	Department of Hippie Studies at New England College offers Ph.D.
2105	Development of gender choice and switching technologies
2106	G-6 emulator with cyberalgorithm for manipulation of feedstocks, both for production on molecular level and for simulation arts and entertainment
2107	United Global Confederacy of 17 continental and subcontinental unions of nations formed
2108	Books with self-mending pages and smart bindings
2109	Pillsbury Library in Warner has new "sim" center
2110	Intoxication science develops Off the Cliff, a faux whiskey with a 30-minute high and no hangover that can be instantly antidoted by Straight
2111-2115	The Army of Urban Poor (TAUP) launches nonviolent campaign for justice
2116	The "new terrorism" in scattered cities from Boston to Santiago; 7,000 die in designer toxic agent attack in American Union administrative capital São Paulo
2117	Amnesty and an end to TAUP uprising and implementation of program of Union Organization for Democracy and Justice
2118	Cultural studies replace social studies in schools
2125	Global murder rate is under 1000 per year
2126	Universities teach wholism, Gaean dynamics, applied catastrophics, biophilia, limitology, consequential limnology
2133	Jovian moon base established
2134	Reply sent to signal from civilization in Haroon System 323 light-years away; answer expected in 646 years
2140	The global network of 50 million cooperatives established
2141	Global population is four billion (after a century of single-child families, cluster families, and group parenting)
2142	Life expectancy 160 years, with expectation of 150 years of active life
2144	Sustainability, peace, and justice are not just election-year slogans.

Why This Book?

I'm writing this book for my son Sam and for his kids, for all our children and grandchildren, and for their kids. I'm writing to make it easier for them to remember where we came from and help shape where we may be going.

For as long as our family can remember, almost three hundred years, back to the nineteenth century in Russia, there's been a Sam Morrison. Sam is from a biblical name, Sh'muel, meaning "asked of G-d" in Hebrew, the fulfillment of a mother's wish.

We learn about history in school as the record of big events, grand themes, about wars and heroes and villains. It's history reduced to statutes in parks and official celebrations. But history's really not like that. History is also what happened to families and their towns.

My family has lived in our small town of Warner, New Hampshire since the twentieth century. After nine generations, maybe we've been here long enough to be considered natives. Maybe not long enough for some who trace their roots to the Mayflower, and certainly not for the Abenaki who lived and thrived here for many, many generations before that.

Today, in the year 2144, when the digitized history of the last 160 years can be sliced, sorted, and recombined to suit individual whims, it's time to take a breath, to step out of the data stream and see the whole forest appearing from the protean materializing data. So I'm writing an old-fashioned straight-ahead book. Images must remain in imagination and be dependent upon unassisted reflection freed from cyber clues and interpretive personal search engines.

Being old-fashioned, I sometimes believe that through our cyber technology we can now know anything, manipulate everything, but understand nothing. So pause, or even dare to sever for an undisclosed period of time, your web connections. Calm the propinquity sensors tying us together. Sit on a rock by the Warner River or the plunging Slaughter Brook or your own riverine retreat and spend a few timeless moments reflecting upon our time of surprising comfort and conditional wealth. Consider with me how and why we have come to this place.

In the past, the sages said that the miracles of science would solve our problems. Others consigned their fate to the invisible hand of the market. Some looked toward deliverance through the influence of divine providence.

At the height of the modern crisis in the mid-twenty-first century, when the survival of civilization, indeed of the human species itself, seemed in doubt, there was no end to the cacophony of competing absolutes offering mutually exclusive paths toward salvation. This was to be expected in a world of wars over resources, global famine, pandemics, mass migrations of the desperate, and inexorable climatic change. In 2050 the end not only seemed to be near, but the catastrophe was in the process of engulfing us.

But we surprised the pessimists and doomsters of the twenty-first century. The mad mullahs and crazed ministers preaching theocratic reaction, the technofascists offering war and the well-ordered world of machines, in fact, virtually the entire conglomeration of the fearful and the desperate became historical artifacts. In the end, we could, and we did, resolve our problems. The old pessimism became the new optimism, after painful and then surprising decades.

We reached the ecological dawn after the long night of industrialism, not by dint of science or revolution, or through grand schemes, or dumb luck. All right, luck did play a part now and then. Every kid learns from his or her parents about the catalysts developed by a young Italian fashion designer who had earned a Ph.D. in chemical engineering before she'd been laid off by Fiat and went to work in the family fashion business. Trying to produce self-cleaning clothes, she generated hydrogen from the solar electrolysis of water in a way that was easier and cheaper than anyone had thought possible. A lucky accident or two (or what could reasonably be attributed to fortune favoring the well-prepared and motivated) aside, we moved decisively in the direction of sustainability that we had been slowly turning toward by fits and starts since at least the middle of the twenty-first century.

We did it by using the tried-and-true tools of our democracy. It wasn't pretty. It wasn't easy, and our success wasn't predestined. We did so because we had no choice and the alternatives were all so much worse. By the early decades of the twenty-second century, when the shape of the great ecological transformation finally became clear, a new American pragmatism clearly had asserted itself.

One hundred years after those contested and afflicted times of the 2040s and 2050s, we still have our problems, to be sure, and grave warnings still surface about the future, but this has become, in comparison, a remarkably staid and self-satisfied time. Ecological principles and ecological conduct have become the new common sense, and have been the new orthodoxy for at least three or four generations. A global industrial civilization has been transformed into what is acknowledged even by its critics, and there are many, to be a global ecological civilization.

Make no mistake. This is still the Live Free or Die state. We're constitutionally—personally, that is, with a small *c*—as out of step as ever with our neighbors. Always were. Still are. Across the Connecticut River in Vermont, sun, sweetness, and light have generally prevailed, at least since the fabled Hippie Migration of the late twentieth century, the so-called harbinger of things to come. Here in the Granite State, certainly to the north of Concord, the state capital, we smile only on occasion. And the occasion had better be a good one.

Concord is now a border town specializing in trade with Massachusetts and the Southern New England Confederacy (SNEC). The SNEC was joined by that strip of twenty-first-century urbanism formerly in New Hampshire, a strip running south of Concord, west of Route 125, and ending east of Milford heading toward Keene. In 2095 they voted in the strip by town to strike the *Don't Tread on Me* flag and change state identities.

The state, New Hampshire, that is, received due consideration for the transfer and thereby resolved another of the its desperate funding crisis, fending off once again a state income tax and maintaining our traditional structural deficit by drawing down both interest and principle from the billions received as state patrimony for the sale. Patrimony was, alas, sacrificed on the altar of expediency, thereby keeping taxes low for the rich.

New Hampshire's ongoing peculiarities aside, some politicians in 2144—although not in Concord—and even some professors are now saying that this almost thoroughly post-postmodern ecological world (in attitude, if not in fact) is now almost a u-topia. What can anyone who can still tell the difference between a cow pie and a potpie say to that? Utopia?

You can still walk into the Warner Cooperative Market on a Sunday afternoon and hear scarcely a word exchanged between or among self-possessed shoppers minding their own business. It's all part of an embrace of our singularity. So, happy or not in the twenty-second century, we're still not acting the way they tell us to.

That's another meaning of *Live Free or Die*. Or, as the meaning's been explained in our family, "New Hampshire's hard, but people leave you alone." If states had an official dog, to the south they'd pick the placid and loving golden retriever. In the Granite State, the dog would be a wily and large mutt of uncertain parentage, but clearly containing more than just splashes of shepherd for brains and strength, black-and-tan hound for hunting and tracking, and terrier for that Jack Russell (I-don't-care) ornery courage.

Forget about utopia. This is still a world of places and peoples and lands with their own aspects and characters in motion, places with a history and an unfolding future subject to the consequences, whether intended or not, of our actions and of things beyond our control. I'm writing from my perspective here, not thinking I can rise up and look down on the world from nowhere and say with perfect and bloodless objectivity what happened and why. So I'm still inside it. I'm here trying to tell you what I think went on, and to help you think about what to do next.

Almost of us, some politicians aside, are smart enough to draw inferences. Otherwise I'd keep bumping my head every morning on the way to the kitchen on that same beam that's sagged too low in the old house. I remember to duck because I live there.

Maybe that caution's a sign of my age and the supposed conservatism that comes with it, the sense from too many lessons that not all things are possible, and that we drag our history with us, like it or not. But I don't see hard life lessons as the basis for a political credo and a brief against change.

Experience, the bruises and all, has fostered, instead of a can't-do attitude, an awareness of the complexity of being rooted in the connections between people and land and history. This is what shaped our past and is affecting our futures. It's a matter of coevolution, however much that too-popular term has been overused and lost its meaning.

As George Santayana cautioned, we have to learn from our past in order not to be condemned to repeat it. Not just remember the past as postcard. But examine and learn from our strengths and weaknesses, our triumphs and defeats. Freedom and community, which is what we've learned to value most and really care about here, have a context. We are not free agents writing on a blank slate. Nor are we prisoners to received wisdom and an unexamined common sense that has lost touch with reality.

What intellectual historians now term the twenty-first-century Era of Eschatologies, or endings, has been replaced in the minds of most, most outside of New Hampshire anyway, as the Age of Contentment. Since *Time* magazine put "Happy Days Again" on the cover, the sentiment has ricocheted around the world, filling space real and cyber with self-satisfied enthusiasm. Today's fashion and cultural statements are packed with references and iconic images paying homage to the allegedly Happy Days of 200 years before, in the 1950s.

That those were also times of racism and xenophobia, a nuclear arms race, an unparalleled acceleration of industrial destruction of habitat and assault upon the environment, the profligate use of natural resources, and a global expansion of poverty and population should give us pause. I'm writing not to cast aspersions on the very real and epochal achievements of this current ecological age, or to disparage the efforts stretching back into the twentieth century of those upon whose work and ideas we have built our current and, we believe, sustainable prosperity.

To intelligently make choices about where we are going, we must understand how we have arrived here, how grave threat and affliction yielded not to the pursuit of endless growth, but the embrace of a sustainable prosperity, of justice and democratic choice. It wasn't easy, and it wasn't entirely an accident. We need to understand why and how.

This then is an assessment, a survivor's journal, to remind our young people, and those who were not paying attention, about from where we came and how we arrived here, and to consider the current state of affairs, so as to gain perspective on how we can continue, to use a now archaic metaphor in this age of cyber travel and mag-lev craft, to build the road as we travel.

The More Things Change . . .

The sap season is ending in Warner, New Hampshire, as the maple buds begin to open with the spring and the sap turns bitter.

Warner's still a mountain hamlet at the edge of the Lakes Region. The great Lake Sunapee is 20 miles to the north. Mount Kearsarge, really just a 3,000-foot-hill, rises steeply and spectacularly to the northeast above Warner village.

I live in the old Morrison homestead in the Mink Hills, a series of small peaks and ridges folded over one another that stretches across the west side of town toward Henniker and Hillsborough. And there are minks again in these hills, and moose and lynx and bobcat and grey wolves, and rare but undeniable sightings of cougars ranging southward from the Whites. And Henniker's still the only Henniker on earth.

Warner's population is just around 2,000 now, about what it was 200 years ago in 1950, down from a peak of nearly 4,000 in 2020.

The Bowers are finishing up another good year on their Kearsarge Mountain Farm. It's a heritage organic farm, having been registered organic since certification began in the late twentieth century.

The farm also has the distinction of having used solar electricity from the start. Founders Jennifer Ohler and Bob Bower, farmers and sustainable loggers, used only early photovoltaic arrays to wring small amounts of solar power from the daylight. Nary a power line ever snaked its way into the Kearsarge Gore high on the northwest side of the mountain.

Bob and Jennifer built their organic renaissance farm and resurrected its fields from an old 400-acre woodlot that once upon a time had been a farm, embracing the hard, hard everyday work of getting up before dawn and often laboring until after the sun had gone down.

They built their sap house and began boiling sap to supplement their income soon after they started farming. In those days, back in the twentieth century, it was still buckets hung on trees. Soon it was various incarnations of plastic piping leading to collection tanks. That lasted nearly a century. Now it's small in-line photovoltaically powered pumps sending the sap to the collection tank from smart taps that open or close depending on the volume of the flow, the sugar concentration in the sap, and the age and health of the tree.

From 2030 to 2050, as the climate warmed dramatically, sap production declined rapidly, and finally ceased for all practical purposes, as the great die-off of maple trees on the mountain accelerated. The Bowers' grandkids and great-grandkids replanted the mountain with 50,000 maple seedlings in 2070 as the climate began to stabilize, and those trees began producing sap for maple syrup again 40 years ago; over the last 20 years production has become something like normal again.

As a renaissance farmer practicing sustainable agriculture and agro-forestry, Sam Bower can afford to finish his syrup in the classic wood-fired evaporator. Selective reverse osmosis concentrates syrup about 90 percent of the way from sap, at a bit more than 8 pounds a gallon, to syrup, at 11 pounds a gallon.

And the wood-fired finish, when the golden liquid flows in the pans and then through the opened money tap, is both a spring ritual marking communal survival after another winter and a reenactment of the old ways for the tourists and customers, as well as a way to add just that little bit of smoky undertaste.

Sam is able to charge customers the lowest of the ecological value-added taxes (EVATs), the A rate of 15 percent, on his syrup.

Without the sustainable forestry investment in smart taps and solar-powered reverse osmosis, his tax rate could soar to C, D, or even an E, a 75–125 percent sales tax on his syrup that would effectively put him out of business.

Ecological taxation came easy in New Hampshire, where there never was and still isn't a statewide income tax. It made sense when the ecological changes came to phase out all taxes on income with ecological sales taxes on pollution, depletion, and ecological destruction. The more polluting, the higher the tax. When you shopped, the cheaper item would be the one that was the most ecologically sustainable.

As every school kid learns today: "If the market rules are right, the price points the way." And: "A smart market means you can do well and do good."

Sam's daughter Phoebe runs the network part of the Kearsarge Gore Farm business. She's able to sell native producer's royalty rights over the net. Many people of the Central African Union, one of the 17 continental and subcontinental democratic unions of nations that make up the United Global Confederacy, have a taste for maple syrup, which goes particularly well with their own palm wine.

Instead of shipping product halfway around the world, Phoebe can sell information, the code for her syrup, to be formulated by nanotech zero emissions—zero-waste organic production systems. And Warnerites have begun developing a fashionable taste for palm wine during our own celebrations. In the twenty-second century, we usually move information, in general, not things, across the world.

Last month was a wonderful transcontinental virtual celebration connected over the net as we danced in the fields to the music of banjo and guitars from here and drums and stringed instruments from a field along a river in Africa.

The underlying production principles, of course, are zero emissions, zero waste, and sustainable use of organic chemical feedstocks. *Organic* has become a twenty-second-century play on words; it's both a natural farming technique and the source of the organic chemicals that were once derived from petroleum and fossil fuels.

Local organic farmers grow the ubiquitous mustard plant, hemp, Jerusalem artichokes, and alder that the Warner Farmers' Co-op makes into chemical feedstocks. We grow much of what we manufacture. In the popular "sims," a character who's imbibed a bit too much palm wine advises a friend's son, in classic movie homage, "Ben, let me tell you just one word you need to know about your future. Mustard. Enough said."

Mustard's new career began in Warner in the early twenty-first century as global oil production peaked and the great energy price inflation began. The scientists at the University of New Hampshire, led by chemical engineer Ahab Farrag, realized that the ubiquitous small seed of yellow mustard was a perfect source of biodiesel fuel, made from the oil pressed from the seeds. You'd combine vegetable oil with alcohol and a catalyst, and end up with biodiesel fuel and glycerine as a by-product. The pressed mustard seed paste was used to make an organic insecticide. The rest of the plant was made into ethanol. The glycerin was used for organic soaps. The ash residue was an organic fertilizer to spread on the fields.

Abandoned pastures began to be covered in fields of yellow mustard, a vigorous and prolific plant not far removed from its native ancestor. The Bowers grew acres of it, under a contract between the farmer's co-op and Stonyfield Farm, the organic yogurt maker in Londonderry. The mustard seed oil was turned into biodiesel to replace the hundreds of thousands of therms of natural gas used to make the yogurt, heat the plant, and generate electricity. The carbon dioxide generated by burning was equal to the carbon dioxide sequestered by its growth. The biodiesel wasn't just climate neutral. Yellow mustard biodiesel proved to meet the triple-bottom-line test of sustainability: on the economic, ecological, and social levels. The farmers, processors, and users all made money. The local and planetary ecology was protected. Local communities were strengthened.

It wasn't perfect, of course. We were still producing (NOX) from combustion, but we were moving on the right road and developed necessary catalysts. The ecological tax structure made that a nobrainer.

The Warner Farmer's Co-op eventually built their own biodiesel plant in conjunction with other regional farmers' groups and the workers' co-op that operated the plant. Closing the gap between industrial production and ecology ultimately meant closing the gap between political and economic power.

We not only had a stake in the outcome of industrial conduct; we had a democratically controlled economic stake in the matter. We had seats at the table. In the long run, ecological sustainability rested on the expansion of democracy from the political into the economic realm. Our sustainable and ecological twenty-second-century world rests on a base of justice and fairness. Our success is a further confirmation of the wisdom of Tom Jefferson and the Founders when practiced in light of twenty-second-century realities. That was one of the most pleasant surprises. We knew what to do all along. We just had to do it.

Warner likes its traditions. It's a small town with four museums, a college, and an institute. The Warner Indian Museum was started in the 1990s by Bud Thompson on the Mountain Road after he retired from running Shaker

Village in Canterbury, a few years after the death of the last of the original Shakers, Eldress Bertha.

Bob Bower also, in what he called his working retirement in the 2020s, founded the experiential Museum of the American Hippie, at the edge of a hay field not too far from his sap house and farm pond, where there'd been periodic music gatherings and a growing unofficial graveyard for VW buses, a collection of tepees, and other vintage but still-used paraphernalia. The museum began as a tongue-in-cheek sign Bob cut with a router and hung on a tree where the unmaintained class 6 road leading to the farm at the edge of the Gore began.

Now the museum has a curator and interns from Magdalene College down the Mountain Road majoring in ecological ethics.

And there's been a Sam Bower in Warner along with a Sam Morrison since the 1990s. Bob and Jennifer named their son Sam, claimed local rights to what was to become a popular name for a time, and were somewhat annoyed when Sam Morrison was born. "We'll call him Sh'muel," Jennifer would say, according to a passage in a long narrative poem, *The Loggers of Warner*, about late-twentieth-century Warner, whose first edition, with Bob Bower on the cover, is still in the Pillsbury Free Library downtown in the village.

Yes, "V-books," virtual books, with sensory enhancement switched on or off at your pleasure, are the everyday thing. But there's still nothing like an old paper volume with its unique, not simulated texture and feel and smell. Unenhanced imagination and the writer's words can do the trick. The sound of a chainsaw and the smell of cut wood don't need to accompany the words in what I find to be an insulting and annoying kind of background score.

Yes, that too can be a high art in the hands of a genius compositor like Mark Awodey or Lester Hirsh. When I want that, I go to the compositor section of the data net. When I want to read a book, I sometimes, old fogy that I am, can get one that is free, and already read a couple of hundred times, from the library.

I'm still a reality-monger after all these years. And for me at least, that's changed from a snide teenage putdown of thirty years ago to a bit of satisfying self-evaluation—like the way Yankee Doodle moved the American revolutionary army.

Now it's true that real books wear out, even twenty-second-century books with self-mending pages and smart bindings. And then, being a reality-monger means to have the book become part of the feedstock for the library's emulator, which will produce a faithful copy of the original from the database.

Is it original or is it emulated? This question provides a popular pastime for experts, since the copies are identical on the chemical and molecular level and are also manipulated by cyber-algorithm to approximate degrees of newness, uniformity, and wear. An early tipoff in the game was that copies at first were too good, too similar, and without the minor variations of conventional production. The current G-6 emulator is a very sophisticated machine indeed, combining modules for intelligence, judgment, sensory perception, with a sense of art and humor, finding them to be integrally interdependent as the allegedly smarter G-5 machine discovered.

As they say, don't even think about messing with a G-6 emulator. It will change a line of your flawless copy from "Do not go gentle into that good night" to "Revenge is a dish best served cold."

When the Pillsburys endowed the town library in the nineteenth century, they had the good sense to condition their gift on the basis of a town warrant article providing one-quarter of one percent of town tax revenues for the library in perpetuity. Not too long ago, the 350th Warner Town Meeting funded a state-of-the-art simulation, or sim, center for the twenty-second-century library to make it a focus for youth activities and creativity to balance daring athleticism at the Hover Skate Park near the Warner River with artistic and intellectual adventures.

We still vote in the old Town Hall, with provisions made for distanced participation by those too old or too sick to make it down to town. The warrant is still printed, but the rest of the town report, with data and town departments offering reports, sim-dramas, and data, is distributed over the web to everybody's personal computer or personal communicator (and web link computer).

Town Meeting

At Town Meeting in Warner, a member of the Courser family still sits, as is traditional, in the first row on the left. Rebecca Courser, who bears the name of Warner's celebrated town historian, still makes clear her feelings on the misleading and lugubrious flow of the meeting and is counted on "to call the question" with aplomb.

About the same number of people, more or less, as they always have, fill the Town Hall for the meetings. Some come early and take seats near the front. Others resolutely stand along the walls. Some enjoy the sight above the fray from the balcony looming over the hall below, where their voices boom down, *deus ex machina.*

Our culture and its ways endure. Albion's roots set down into this hard and rocky land took hold over the centuries, and the settler heritage of the English immigrants still endures to shape and alter wave upon wave of new migrants, and disparate cultures are as much absorbed into the New England bean pot as they subtly and not so subtly transform it or attempt to do so. It's still a hard land with hard people, for whom the state motto, *Live free or die*, is more than an antique battle cry of eighteenth-century patriots. Private wisdom passed down from mother to daughter and father to son is of the practical side of *Live free or die*, with its implicit grant of a kind of lonely tolerance, toughness, and pride.

That pride and the shame over the outrages perpetrated in the early twenty-first century, it's said, caused the state's Old Man in the Mountain to come plunging down into the valley floor one day in 2004, never to rise again, despite periodic attempts at resurrection, literal or virtual.

Those plans would eventually all fail, despite copious expenditures on boosterism and tourist promotion, when the absurdity of a synthetic Old Man would be pointed out, sometimes from the most unlikely sources, whether rock-ribbed conservative curmudgeon or sensitive liberal.

It was believed, at least for a few serious weeks and then for some tongue-and-cheek months, that your visage, for a price, could temporarily grace the new holographic Old Man. This would, it was argued, fund Fish and Game's trophy trout project in its entirety and really do no harm either to migratory geese, the Canon Mountain raptor rookery, or our dignity, which we all admitted was not for sale, no matter what some fool would pay to have their face shone onto a mountain. But it never happened.

The battle over the new Old Man was, in its way, an exemplar of the struggle over the emerging ecological imperative. What was too phony would not and could not be expected to endure in our collective names. So while many people were more than just mildly surprised, in the end it was *Live free or die* New Hampshire that led the way in the movement toward ecological sustainability, and not environmentally conscious and liberal-leaning Vermont. Lacking nuance and liberalism, New Hampshire was less handicapped in eventually adapting to the realities of the twenty-first century that became all too apparent.

And town meeting, that most archaic and singular New Hampshire institution, emerged as the linchpin of the ecological changes that emerged from below and bubbled up through the American political scene and beyond in response to the seemingly intractable problems of the Great Industrial Crisis. It was town meeting resolutions, for instance, that first definitely said no to more resource wars for oil and for water, much as town meetings did nearly 100 years before in the twentieth century, when they passed resolutions calling for a nuclear freeze and an end to the nuclear arms race. And the town meeting spirit of local reconstruction and renaissance went on from there.

We are still hearing the same motions that Rebecca gathered from old warrants and minutes from the nineteenth and twentieth centuries, let alone the twenty-first, for a transition to a more *efficient* and professional administrator-assisted town council and a mayor instead of three selectmen. Efficiency, of course, without concern for consequences, is the handmaiden of industrialism and injustice and the enemy of democracy and sustainability.

Speed is not a reliable measure of efficacy, and it is certainly anathema to the sometimes wonderful alchemy of direct democracy that occasionally, not always, happens at town meeting when the town decisively and profoundly gets things right.

In 2073 in Warner, for instance, the town finally decided not simply to pass resolutions, as significant as they sometimes are, about sustainability expressing the sense of the town and instructing our legislators in Concord, Washington, Montreal, and São Paulo. Nor did the Town Meeting just attempt to legislate using the authority granted us under law and the Rio Treaty of 2062 for local self-management and ecological self-protection.

In 2073 the Town Meeting decided that the town would not just opine, legislate, or direct but would act creatively and entrepreneurially in the interest of sustainability and prosperity for our land and our families. "The action is here!"

The twenty-second-century Town Meeting is about more than just passing budgets and deciding when we need new pieces of ever more expensive fire and safety equipment. We now deal with yearly changes and developments in the town sustainability plan. And Town Meeting is also the annual meeting of Warner Community Enterprises, where the yearly business and sustainability plans produced by its component co-ops—the school, housing, child and elder care, and enterprise community cooperatives—are discussed and voted on, in the third day of the meeting.

As is traditional, on day 1, the polls are opened in the Town Hall for voting on ballot items. They're still on paper and still counted by hand, as they've been for 350 years. The reality-mongers have beaten back attempt after attempt to use machines instead of people to count ballots in the town; it has decided that participation, not efficiency, matters more.

Day 2 deals with the town warrant, and on day 3, as it has done since the later twenty-first century, the town considers and votes on the yearly business and sustainability plans of the community cooperatives. We've become an ownership, enterprise, and stewardship town. We don't just own private property, our homes, our land, and our small businesses. We are also owners of town social property, our community schools, housing, and other institutions, and our community cooperative enterprises, where many of us work. We run things by a one-member, one-vote system.

The question of the day is how do we strike a balance between the desire of the organic farmers to have more fields for mustard and hemp to supply the nano plant and the imperatives not to upset the wild lands of the Chandler Reservation. The reservation maintains the fine balance between woodland predator and prey, and keeps bears and coyotes mostly out of our backyards. The answer today was to expand membership of the co-op to include new Henniker farmers who are reclaiming abandoned twentieth-century subdivisions for farming along the Mink Hills border.

The community cooperative businesses are Warner businesses owned by and run by the people of Warner. And they are run to be both profitable and sustainable. And while it seems redundant to say profitable and sustainable, they are still not the same things. Our twenty-second-century market rules, an ecological tax structure, and a business finance system catalyzed and led by the Union Trust does profoundly incline market activity and profitability toward sustainability. Nonetheless, subtle but real diversions between the two still exist.

Over time, unless corrected for the effect of such small differences, small differences can prove to be profound, like an ancient earth calendar missing a leap year, or a Jovian moon base with a day just a fraction of a minute off from a 24-hour rotation. Over decades the old calendar's months and seasons diverged, and today on Jupiter's moons our human circadian rhythms, our earthly sense of night and day, become profoundly disoriented after a couple of months of days that are just 15 seconds too short.

The corporation of the nineteenth, twentieth, and twenty-first centuries, based on absentee investor stock ownership and professional managerial buccaneers, was an artifact of history and the pursuit of self-interest, not an expression of divine providence. By its nature, the stock corporation was the progenitor of industrial ecological pillage and social injustice not human liberation and happiness. Of course, it wasn't meant to be this way.

What was missing, however, right from the start, was ethics. Ethics was precisely what Adam Smith himself understood in his discussion of "moral sentiments" as essential to the operation of markets to serve the public good. Smith's vision of a market where personal acquisitiveness conditioned by ethics would maximize public benefit was transformed to a market where greed alone, in the view of the greedy and their sycophants, was believed to be sufficient motivation toward the development of the best of all possible worlds.

A little history lesson is called for to remind of us of things we should not forget about the trajectory of untempered acquisitiveness and power. In the late eighteenth and early nineteenth centuries, the nascent capitalist class, the holders of private wealth available for the new industrial businesses, competed for power with the then dominant aristocracy of land and privilege. The landed lords had little interest in investing in the mysterious "satanic mills" and not in the land, livestock, and sometimes slaves that had been the root of their prosperity and power. Eventually, the landlords lost. The new capitalist class, rising to ascendance along with their stock companies, supplanted their power.

The industrial capitalist system, with its stock corporations, rose over time to global dominance, and also devolved over time into a casino capitalism driven by financial manipulation and the maximization, by any means necessary, of quarterly earnings reports. This was the twenty-first-century world, where cleaning up an oil spill or a nuclear accident was regarded as a productive and profitable use of resources.

The life of the stock company was shaped by and co-evolved with the underlying imperatives of the industrial system to maximize production and consumption, power and private profit. Profits soared; the earth sickened. The private profit of corporations was more than offset by the true costs of pollution, depletion, and ecological pillage not booked into the corporate balance sheets. The planet was becoming progressively impoverished. And the rich and powerful, attended by a claque of bought-off experts and public relations flacks, pretended not to notice. The band played on. And the earth bled. The skies wept.

By the mid-twenty-first century, it had become all too clear that we could no longer afford to pay the true costs in subsidies and ecological pillage wrought by the universe of stock corporations in the name of private wealth. The great bailouts of the 2030s and 2040s after the failure of the banking and oil industries, following the definitive collapse of the ability of OPEC to revive oil supplies to meet demand, made the costs of industrial business as usual too great to continue to willingly bear it.

The cooperative and community-based corporation, as the new ascendant business model, developed along with the adoption of ecological market rules and the cry for "no more bailouts" and "taxpayers' rights." The requirement to pay the true costs of production arose with the inability to shift costs to society at large or to future generations. This was not an expression of high-mindedness or good governance. We had no other choice. It was change or die; change or progressive impoverishment. We were both eating and poisoning our seed corn. It had to stop.

And it also "suddenly" became clear that the preponderance of financial resources were in institutional hands in the name of worker's pensions and in government securities and investments. New ecological fiduciary rules made the wisdom of investment in co-ops and community corporations enticing.

Over time, the essential choice turned out not to be between corporate or state ownership and control, between a discredited industrial capitalism and a discredited industrial socialism. Rather, the meaningful choice was between economic direct democracy, based on one person, one vote, and absentee corporate ownership, based on one dollar, one vote. Eventually democracy and the pursuit of freedom and community prevailed over the practices of the self-destructive lords of industrial capital.

The Fortune 500 as measure of corporate glory was supplanted by the Cooperative 50,000. And yes, I know there are large second- and third-degree cooperatives of global significance. But these cooperatives, whose members are other co-ops, are not the co-op replacement for corporate behemoths. They are service enterprises that exist to assist their members and whose elected management is also capable of exercising strategic initiatives, as well as forming new virtual and shifting alliances as a whole and facilitating the same actions by its members. That's the power of the global network economy. It's protean. It's democratic to its core. It's community based. It's empowered and entrepreneurial to its bones.

And it's proven not just to be fair and democratic. It's both more efficient and more durable. The cooperative system has flattened the capitalist business cycle of boom and bust. The cooperative global network economy rests on the redundant power and transparency of distributed networks. The open source, open access, common standards movement that maximizes creativity and transparency feeds a network of 50 million active cooperative participants constantly responding to one another. The Microsoft world of the twenty-first century oligopoly and the heavy corporate dancers has gone the way of the feudal lord and the nation-state. The twenty-second century has been called the era of no brand.

The world of the 50 million cooperatives is a world of open competitive markets, shaped by ecological and cooperative rules eliminating the inherently unstable and self-destructive conduct of secretive, giant corporate oligopolies that attempted to maximize profits at the expense of both one another and their customers and workers. The ecological market rules make price reflect true costs. The cooperative market rules dampen down the business cycle and human misery. The network economy maximizes efficiency, information, and productive activity. Joseph Schumpeter's capitalist process of creative destruction has become the process of cooperative reconstruction.

The community, not the corporation, has come to be seen as the essential molecule of economic life, composed of the atoms of various sorts of community-based cooperatives. And communities and their residents evolve and change according to circumstances in accord with democratic, cooperative, and ecological norms. They are not destroyed like fungible piles of corporate assets to be bought and sold and disposed of along with their workers.

In the cooperative world, unemployment is the last, not the first, recourse of business. Transfers, retraining, time sharing, and job sharing—the whole range of opportunities is pursued. Yes, community cooperatives as business entities can and sometimes do fail. But far more often the nature of the cooperative network economy means that first, they change.

The community cooperative has two formal designations: it is either *community-based* or *community-owned*. In theory, and in the practice of large communities, community-based cooperatives can operate largely independently of local government. For example the Green Bay Packers, once again Global Bowl champs, is a most venerable community-based cooperative owned by residents of Green Bay, the majority of whom are descendants of the original cooperators. The cooperative owners hire the general manager, who hires staff and players. Staff and players are also cooperative members with representation on the cooperative's board and receive a share of the profits.

As has become customary, there is also a board seat for customers, in this case season ticket holders, since they've purchased all the seats. Season ticket holders do not have to be cooperative members. Co-op membership is voluntary, but the voice of stakeholders is recognized and heard.

The cooperative has longtime and profound formal and informal connections to the city of Green Bay, which has various business relationships with the cooperative and its subsidiary enterprises but does not directly participate in cooperative governance. And the cooperative has not over its history received funds, either loans or an equity investment, from the American Trust.

Other community cooperatives have partial town ownership and investment, and some are completely town owned. In Warner, the Reuse Co-op is one of the few managed directly by the town, which holds the majority of equity, the rest being held by employees as long as they are working. Reuse Co-ops are typically municipally controlled enterprises, since they involve the participation of almost everyone in the town in their operation.

The Nano Tech Enterprises Co-op, on the other hand, has a town equity stake, but is owned by a combination of the farmers who grow organic feedstocks, the customers who contract for production, the owner-workers, and the town. Nano Tech itself is part of a larger service cooperative that provides materials and high-technology support for its members. This sort of second-degree, multimember cooperative that achieves economies of scale (if they exist to serve and coordinate operation of member enterprises) effectively replaced over time the destructive industrial corporate giants of the twentieth and twenty-first centuries.

The cooperative market economy proved over time to be efficient, that is, responsive to ecological market rules and signals; democratic—based on one person, one vote instead of one dollar, one vote; and sustainable. For community-based enterprises, the wrestling with questions of sustainability was quite stark, simply because there was much less separation between worker-owners and the consequences of their activities in their communities. Why we shouldn't piss in our own wells became a quite clear decision.

Over time, a full retinue of effective cooperative and community-based financial and investment instruments and governance techniques were developed to effectively supplant the stock-based corporation and its stock markets. The rise of the web demonstrated early in the twenty-first century, with the ascendancy of Google, that stock ownership could be routinely separated from control in the interest of long-term development; the way toward sustainability and prosperity was the closing of the gap over time between ownership, employment, community, and democracy.

The effective twenty-second-century cooperative corporation has internalized and substantially eliminated the disparity of interests among owners, workers, and communities. Workers are owners and community members. They profit on the basis of their own labor while they are working. They cannot sell the co-op and profit on the basis of future earnings and labor of future workers. When they retire, they are no longer voting members. They receive a fair share of the co-op's profits when they are employed.

In practice, particularly with participation, under the auspices of the town, of local sustainable economic development co-op corporations (SEDCCs) in financing and fundraising and sustainable development planning, the difference between community-owned and community-based cooperatives is not drawn with a bright line. There are community-based cooperatives that appear to be more entwined with town decision-making and governance than are some town-owned cooperatives that operate rather independently, having been given grants of authority from the town.

In Warner, since the town was small, our local SEDCC, for historical reasons, was set up as a town entity to invest in local business, selling shares to anyone but limiting voting to Warner residents. The Warner SEDCC became a part equity owner and not just a debt financier of Warner Sustainable Forest Products, Warner Eco-Industries, Kearsarge Informatics, Sundance Solar, and Mink Hills Renewable Energy. It's a small town, and the entrepreneurial energies that went into the SEDCC were those of many of the same people who were participants and principals in the cooperatives.

So, even though in formal terms the third day of Town Meeting is the official annual meeting of the SEDCC and the Warner town-based cooperatives, they are understood in meaning and in spirit to be part of the Town Meeting and our identity and action as a town. What happens in the business section of the meeting effects all of us in the most profound and fundamental ways.

The twentieth-century sense of separation of democracy and economy no longer obtains in the twenty-second-century. This realization was an artifact of hard-won common sense that made it essential for us to understand the convergence and interrelationship between democracy and economy and not allow either to function in a way that endangered the other.

So it's an ongoing dance between conflicting, but ultimately harmonizing, perspectives. And the ends and means for that have been town meeting and old-fashioned New England direct democracy, where we all have our say and cast our votes. And of course part of this is the well-crafted sense of what can be voted on and how it must be warned in the warrant, how even the exercise of the purest of democracy's forms must be well tempered and limited, much as the exercise of our business acumen must be well tempered and limited by imperatives for sustainability and democracy.

Rebecca is once again on her feet and in her laconic and bright voice, calling the question . . .

Freedom and Community

Warner is a self-managing and entrepreneurial community. We're more dynamic and prosperous than some and more laid-back than others, attentive to the everyday pleasures of the woods, rivers, and mountains, as well as to the allure of enterprise.

Nonetheless, like the plethora of other twenty-second-century communities, we are tied together in the global network economy and govern ourselves within the context of the American Union of Nations that stretches from the Arctic Confederation of the far north to the far south of Tierra del Fuego in Chile.

What's wonderful about the successful elaboration of the Age of Ecology is the complexity, strength, and diversity of the local, and the web of interconnections that tie it to the larger world. These links have made the existence and nature of the larger framework of structures and institutions within which we live, to a large extent, if not invisible at least simply integral to our daily lives. We don't have to talk much about freedom and community. We live it. Everyday practice is an expression of our ecological principles manifest in the conduct of our lives.

In the twenty-first century decades of crisis, the question of the interdependence of freedom and community was a central issue. The two were not antagonists, as twentieth-century propagandists of both the Right and the Left loudly maintained—to the ultimate detriment and, in fact, near extinction of both freedom and community along with humanity.

Right and Left variously exalted either freedom, identified with the capitalist market, against community, identified with the socialist state, or embraced community, as the well-managed state, against the depredations of freedom, identified as the capitalist market. The decades of crisis that set the stage for the ecological reformation in the twenty-first century and its consolidation in the twenty-second century demonstrated all too copiously and conclusively that you could not have freedom without the supportive and balancing structures of community, and that community without freedom withers under the imposition of tyranny.

What in the twenty-first century represented the Great Political Reawakening was in fact quite traditional and old news, if we'd paid attention to our Founders and revolutionary foremothers and forefathers. *E Pluribus Unum—From Many One*—is written on the ribbon in the mouth of the eagle on the Great Seal of the United States. What was controversial was to remember what that meant in times of trouble when the old ways of greed and growth without limits threatened both prosperity and survival and we needed to change. Or else.

As Tom Paine wrote over 350 years ago, when viewing the emerging revolutionary crisis, "These are the times that try men's souls." And as the American revolutionaries responded to the threats to their lives and liberty by establishing a new democratic order, we responded to the time of war and ecological catastrophe with a series of institutional changes that restored and revivified our Founders' eighteenth-century visions with a new democratic ecological order from a twenty-second-century perspective. As it was for the Founders, the elements that conjoined to build the framework for an ecological civilization were not a matter of organizational charts of the exertions of experts.

No, the sustainability and prosperity of our twenty-second century was built through collective, inspired, and democratic responses to threat and necessity. We were like the Founders, having "to pledge our lives, our fortunes, our sacred honor" to the often daunting tasks at hand. This time we did not just have to defeat an empire to gain our freedom, and agree among ourselves as to the best way to conduct our democracy.

Freedom and community would find new expression through the pursuit of sustainability. The reality of the ecological crisis imposed stern tests upon our democracy and demanded that we follow different paths from the tired industrial norms of growth and greed in the expression of our freedom and our understanding of community.

The creative struggles of America's Founders provided a most useful guide. Their eighteenth- and early nineteenth-century task cast a clarifying light upon our twenty-first- and twenty-second-century efforts. They were wrestling both with attaining and guaranteeing freedom from imperial tyranny and nurturing a framework of communities and institutions that would protect freedom and allow it to thrive.

The Ecological Transformation was a time of the revival of interest in the work, writings, and insights of America's disparate Founders. The debates and realizations of both Federalist and anti-Federalist republicans shone bright lights upon the struggles to create a new, creative, and revivifying balance between freedom and community, between growth and restraint, between ends and means.

The stalwart integrity of Washington, the wisdom of Franklin, the decentralist genius of Jefferson, the financial ledgerdemain of Hamilton, the structural insights of Madison, the political courage of Adams, the truth-telling and boldness of Paine offered across the centuries a clarifying wisdom and insights that were applicable to current circumstances. We were able to use the heartfelt plans and debates of the past to help create new pathways for a different future.

As Washington said in 1782 at a time of peril to the nation, "You will give one more distinguished proof of unexampled patriotism and patient virtue, rising superior to the pressure of the most complicated sufferings."

We were able to understand in our times, as the Founders did in theirs, that the great task facing our democracy was neither a false choice between freedom *or* community, or between liberty *or* order. Rather, in the twenty-first and twenty-second centuries, the challenge for American democracy was to have and nurture *both* freedom *and* community.

Sustainability as a guiding concept was subsumed under the Founders' understanding of the central concern for democracy of maintaining dynamic balance between freedom and community. The twenty-second century became not an era of regulation or prohibition but of innovation and a new birth of freedom and community.

Balance of freedom and community in dynamic motion was progenitor to the tools and techniques by which we pursued sustainability. Sustainability became manifest in our twenty-second century through an intelligent melding of ecological market rules, investment, community and cooperative entrepreneurship, and a negative income tax.

Sustainability was always more than just the ability to keep physically doing tomorrow what we are doing today by turning back the tide of pollution, depletion, and ecological pillage. That ecological challenge was true enough. But the challenge was always political in its dynamics and rooted in the dynamic relationship between our freedom and our community.

Sustainability is not something to be achieved and then put in a box or a rule book or codified by law. Sustainability is ever in motion, ever a matter for disputation and democratic debate and for sometimes hard choices. What we decide about the Mink Hills, beyond resisting attempts of rapacious development, was always and is always a matter of balancing sometimes complementary and sometimes competing ends.

Sustainability exists in the contact of the now and the next. The context is of efficacy and quality; the measure of quality is *enough*, as opposed to the industrial *more*. Sustainability need not be placid. Indeed, it often rests on the knife edge of contingency, equilibrated by democracy, and held in place for the moment by limits, but ever threatened with tumbling down toward a new and dire equilibrium.

The secret of sustainability is adaptation and feedback, of intelligent coevolution where human action is consciously directed and changed. The industrial model is *We act, the living world adapts*. The sustainable model is of a convergence and harmonizing of patterns of change where human action is no longer held to be an independent or semi-independent variable. We think, we feel, we act, we observe, we react.

Systems analysis in our sustainable twenty-second-century combines the art of the chess master understanding the effects of action, now projected over the multifarious consequences unfolding over several moves ahead, with the wordless insight of a shaman in trance consulting the spirit, weighing the ineffable, and feeling the past, present, and future together in dreamtime. Sustainability is an art, not just a science.

Sustainability is a science of wholes, not just of parts. It's predicated on an understanding of relationships whose outcomes involve an interactive series of conventional and chaotic dynamics, of quantum and Newtonian mechanics, of processes reliably measured and others limited by uncertainty and at best stochastic resolution. But this understanding of a complex stew of dynamics is not the crafting of a very, very complex computer program where data comes in and human action comes out.

Sustainability is about more than predicting the global climate given particular human effluent depredations and modifying our poison production. Sustainability is about actions, reactions, and consequences. Variables in a coevolving system are held to be both dependent and independent, in constant flux, including human social, economic, and political action as both cause and effect.

So, for example, the impact of writing more computer code for human genome synthesis to trade it as electronic information with people in other sustainable communities on the renewable resource–powered web is, by itself, innocuous. What is done with that information, of course, is not. It matters very much indeed if we are making useful human somatic genetic changes with that information. For example, it matters whether we are simply encouraging the nerves in Parkinson's disease to regenerate, or fundamentally changing human heredity in ways that will swiftly escape the vision of the most perceptive chess master and lead the shaman to warn of a strange new land past the mountain with hints of desolation.

I sit here at age 96, now middle-aged, enjoying my extended prime. Still playing basketball in the older men's league. I'm not as quick as I was, but I still have my driving hook and baseline jumper. That is made possible through genetic somatic therapy that has reset the speed of my aging clock and enhanced protein synthesis and immune system durability, combined with stem cell treatment for regeneration and herbal essence treatments. Bilberry for the eyes, hawthorn for the circulation, milk thistle for the liver . . . you get the idea. Together that's made us long-lived and substantially degenerative disease–free, given assiduous pursuit of the health regimen.

The consequences, of course, of the longer life span have been a more enduring commitment to sustainability, more patience, and, along with a smaller population and more older people, fewer kids and many, many more elders. But these are healthy people, not torpid old farts. At least that's what I think. And a 100-year-old woman can still serve, in theory, as surrogate mother for an implanted embryo. For decades the practice has been socially and legally beyond the pale, except in the cases where a daughter cannot conceive and where there are medical reasons that mediate against blended heredity. I say, just because you can do a stupid thing that doesn't mean you should. Sustainability needs to be informed by good sense.

Cluster families, blended heredity, and village and neighborhood parenting have emerged as evolving responses to the nuclear family as the basic reproductive, social, and economic unit. Increasingly popular among groups of friends is genetic implantation of a blended embryo and a variety of shared child-rearing arrangements. This is often, but not always, combined with a shared sexuality among partners.

Fewer kids have meant that they are more cherished or more bothered, more special or more spoiled. Children's rights vis-à-vis aging parents is now a thriving legal subspecialty. Writs of mandamus have been filed by kids, under the advice of their attorneys, to constrain the action of generations of parents, grandparents, great-grandparents, and great-great-great grandparents to stop them from further meddling with the child.

There are still plenty of two-parent couples with one or two kids, more rarely three. In twenty-second-century style, the genders are shuffled like cards in a deck: hetero, homo, transgendered. For some it's now fashionable to switch genders, and for some it has been accomplished twice. My friend Bill on Collins Road became the woman Billie, and now 40 years later he's William again. Go figure. Ego, curiosity, desire, and the resourcefulness of plastic surgeons has still not flagged. We have not seen everything yet.

The world's population peaked at around nine billion in the mid-twenty-first century; there are now about four billion of us. The target is between one and two billion within another two or three centuries. One billion people strikes many as the right amount for long-term sustainability. Of course, the absolute number is less important that what that billion does.

The convergence seems to be upon a durable material culture within healthy renewing ecosystems and a human society whose energies focus on art, knowledge, and play in a dizzying number of combinations and incarnations. The sustainable world has more time, fewer people, less need for things, more spirit.

Fairs, festivals, and the new free-for-alls shape the twenty-second-century imagination, not wars, conquests, profit statements. The Happiness Index (HI) has replaced the gross domestic product (GDP) as the popularly intoned statistic. All self-deprecating humor and puns about the HI were very popular indeed when it first emerged from Silicon Valley.

There was and is a serious side to this. It became clear that for us to truly have more, everyone had to have enough. And our *more* needed to be measured in different ways from the industrial world's measures of output that weighed industrial quantities, not qualities. The HI encompassed matters such as access to clean water, healthy food, education, adequate housing and went beyond these to decidedly nonmaterial measures of human well-being as art opportunities and festival density. The simple mantra of our times became, "For me to have more, everyone must have enough." That was too succinct a statement for those who didn't trust people enough to make sense of what *more* meant, so what's written in schoolbooks these days and projected into the sides of buildings is *For me to have sustainably more, everyone must have enough.*

The unnecessary and unimaginative adjective is a tipoff to a directive issued by a well-intentioned union bureaucrat in Brasilia or Brussels or Johannesburg, ever mindful of our needs, our rights, and responsibilities. Why should I scoff? They choose that necessary work. Better them than me. I'm producing my latest paper book using traditional digital photography for the Museum of the American Hippie. It will combine my compendium of hippie aphorisms applicable to sustainability and photographs of things profoundly hippie, including vintage gear and today's naked hippie youth at play around Bower's Pond.

Much of what drives the HI is the spirit behind the traditional Hippocratic oath, "Do no harm," combined with the prophet Wavy Gravy's injunction, "Don't poop parties." It will all be for sale at the Museum of the American Hippie, renowned for its periodic celebrations and a vacation destination in the flesh for New Englanders or, in emulation, for those around the world. Who would have thought about the existence of a Department of Hippie Studies at New England College offering doctorates for world experts in such specialties as the iconography of the twentieth-century bong?

It's not *necessarily* bad if some interpret the pursuit of happiness in the context of art, knowledge, and play as the accumulation of 20 doctorates earned over a century of nearly ceaseless study uncontaminated by practice. Such were among the unintended consequences of a negative income tax, enhanced healthy life span, and lifetime support for education and training. We've created a new subspecies of library worms, as perpetual students and perpetual scholars proudly describe themselves. Harmless really. And sometimes quite helpful.

There are, of course, counternarratives: of the inherent value of the contemplative and scholarly life of a Talmudic scholar, studying Torah for Torah's sake, and its implication for the nature of that community; of Thoreau's comparison of the value placed on the man spending days on the exchange buying and selling his woods for development compared to the value placed on the supposed idler who spends days walking through those woods watching and thinking.

Sustainability in the broadest sense means we are freed individually and collectively from the whip of want and of material need and given the opportunity to redirect our energies to contemplative, nonmaterial ends, toward art, toward play, toward scholarship and study, toward community, toward social invention.

This is not the distinction of an H. G. Wells between the flesh-eating Molochs, subterranean slaves to the machine, and the beautiful impotent and self-involved Eloi, their decorous prey. Rather, sustainability has meant that the material is very carefully and artfully attended to. But the ecological call for *just enough* and the convergence between means and ends have replaced the ceaseless industrial demand for *more*.

Thus the integration and balancing between work and play. I work at the Museum of the American hippie. I also party at the Museum of the American Hippie. Workaholism is treated as as serious an affliction as alcoholism once was.

I wish that I could have written that drugs, like war, were mostly a thing of the past. Intoxication is usually not part of the tale told by historians and social philosophers. The often profligate drunkenness of the colonialists and of the early United States was a phenomenon well understood but usually accepted as a fact of life, almost like weather, though subject to occasional reformist and moral strictures of prohibitionism.

It's true that in 2144 we often get high by meditating, by stopping our internal dialogue, by being able to really *see* and *hear* the birds and birdsong, the trees and the leaves, by melding with the universe, by sliding into the grand and interlinked space of consciousness and being. More of us do. Meditation is taught along with physical education in schools. And a vision quest in the Mink Hills is part of every kid's coming of age.

Unfortunately, in our twenty-second-century, there are still lost lives, sad children and shattered families. Neither, suasions legal or moral, the transformation of a war on drugs into a program of treatment and education, nor justice and peace as commonplace markers of our world, nor the applied disciplines of meditation, conflict resolution, and peace studies, nor recurring bouts of prohibitionism have done much more than ameliorate aggregate drug use. What has changed is the consequences for most, which has been facilitated by the new class of psychopharmaceuticals. In a transcendently American exercise, drug abuse and addiction has also meant the use of a new class of drugs. Psychopharmaceuticals now ameliorate the use of psychopharmaceuticals.

Drug use today is moderated by a sometimes uneasy combination of social practice assisted by intoxication science. It's not cool to be high in general, and to be an addict and profligate drug user is seen as an expression of psychological problems requiring intervention, even mandatory intervention, since antidotes and designer drug alternatives have made addiction the expression of willful self-destruction that poses a danger not just to oneself but to others.

Drugs are still a matter of social concern. Drugs are also quite pervasively, albeit rather modestly, consumed. The apparently universal human individual and cultural propensity for some kind of intoxication still persists. But the extent and the enormous social and personal costs that were associated in the Industrial Age with the use of drugs, from tobacco to alcohol to opiates to stimulants to hallucinogens, have not altogether vanished.

Given the well-understood biology and biochemistry of intoxication, some still become almost an alcoholic by proxy by consuming Almost faux beer or Off the Cliff faux whiskey. Both have the look, feel, and taste of the real thing, without the major physiological side effects on brain and liver. And both have only a 30-minute-long high and supposedly can be instantly antidoted with, of course, a quick nasal spray of Straight or a tab of Sober dissolved under your tongue. Straight and Sober work for both the faux and the real thing. And with both, you can still have the experience of being sober and incredibly sick to your stomach.

The bar at Tucker's Tavern downtown in Warner mostly sells Almost and

Off the Cliff. Several emerging new competitors, like Smashed and Hammered, have hit the market, as the classics have lost patent protection. The real stuff is still there. But it's almost entirely for show, because the EVAT is very high. So if you want to spend 60 Americans on a shot of Chivas compared to a buck for Off the Cliff, you can.

Smoking is now a mostly retro thing. What passes for a cigarette these days gives you a nicotine related high without the addiction or physiological effects . The smoke itself is lung neutral gas. But that hasn't completely replaced the physical and social attraction of smoking as a habit, a style, and a kind of self-expression. It's a cost and common sense thing that makes smoking ultra low-carcinogen cigarettes a more or less occasional thing for the typical pack-a-month smoker.

Lung cancer, particularly its complications, still occasionally kills people, but you have to work hard at that, given the anti-cancer effects of enhanced immune system somatic gene therapy, cellular screening, and anti-oncologics that have made the growth of tumors, if detected early, a rare thing. The context, of course, is a world substantially free of human-produced carcinogens, to the extent that they are known.

Stimulants, from cocaine to speed, have for generations been out of fashion. Opiates maintain a toehold among those in pursuit of oblivion. But for both, antidotes and non-addictive synthetics have calmed the imperative feeling of *must* that drove addiction and dramatically reduced the self-destructive consequences of use. They've become a sometime practice for a rather small group.

Hallucinogens offer their now-calibrated diversity. Intoxication science has standardized, metered, and personalized a growing range of branded psychedelic offerings, allegedly taking the best from the naturals-marihuana, psilocybin, peyote-and leaving the rest. Your drug of choice has just the desired extent of hallucination and synesthesia, melding color and sound, and you're offered at least a simulacrum of a controlled maybe magical mystery tour through the tripping woods at the museum. Safe and secure. Or so it's proclaimed. A kid did walk off, or slipped off, the edge of a cliff on Kearsarge a few years back with fatal effects.

And, of course, the occasional drunken fool still manages to crash a mag-lev at high speed. This should not happen or even be possible. But it still does, despite the Sober dispenser that by law must be within the operator's reach in all vehicles, despite the technological safeguards against operating while high and the automatic notification of the cops and warnings to other operators, despite collision sensors and automatic crash avoidance, despite the fines and imprisonment and the social sanctions—despite all that, some adventurous fools manage to defeat, disconnect, and subvert redundant safety systems because they like how it feels to move at high speed when drunk, or are really in pursuit of suicide by collision.

Intoxication science, third-generation designer drugs, and antidote availability have not removed the underlying imperative for conscious self-management—or exempted anyone from the consequences of his or her acts. That's what sustainability teaches us. But there I go again, old reality-monger. In fact, our culture, with its emphasis on play and self-expression in all its forms in the context of freedom and community, has paradoxically actually reduced the imperative for escape through intoxication regardless of consequences or in self-destructive pursuit of consequences. The fact that you can be high when you want to be and just when you want to be has meant, as the marketers assure us, that the incidence of intoxication is usually a sometime and recreational thing for most and a careful sacramental thing for some. There's at least some truth in that.

The fundamental flaw with intoxication science is that drug abuse remains, in part, the pursuit not simply of pleasure or the release from pain, but that of a personally crafted cocktail variously in pursuit of escape, oblivion, pleasure, self-destruction, enlightenment. Intoxication science attempts at chemically mediating and moderating desire. But moderation cannot fully satisfy needs that by their nature are anything but measured and straightforward.

For those who find that they just have to be high and can't control themselves, there are the 12-step programs and the broad-spectrum spray-on versions of Straight and Sober that soak into the skin and last a week at a time.

As for an old reality-monger like me, I'm decidedly happy enough to be able to walk through these beautiful woods without chemical enhancement. And then there are the days of the Magic Mushroom Festival, with the classic strains of "Lucy in the Sky with Diamonds" wafting through the summer air above Mount Kearsarge, and I imagine the woods glowing even more intensely before me, if I'd cast my stubborn reality-monger stance aside . . . But ultimately being there and being conscious is what matters.

There were for a while tripping communities made possible by intoxication science. People pursued the orgiastic pleasure of the endless metered high. Their experience was broadly similar to that of the classic communes that flourished in Warner for a time after they began in the 1960s and still thrived occasionally in New Hampshire and more frequently in Vermont throughout the twenty-first century, with a few still continuing today. Drugs by themselves cannot hold a community together. The consistent result is for other pursuits and needs to overtake them, and they become, as they have for native cultures, important and ceremonial activities and much less a daily pursuit, more sacrament than habit, more event than way of life. Life is a trip. But life must be more than just tripping.

Empire

In the twenty-first century, we had to do what has been done before in American history. We had to triumph over empire and business as usual, much as in the nineteenth century we had to prevail over the empire of slavery. In the nineteenth century, the crucial questions were questions of slavery and economics and the nature of our union. In the twenty-first century the questions were of ecology and economics and the nature of our union.

Like the Cotton Kingdom's slave empire of the nineteenth century, the twenty-first century Empire of Oil had to continue to expand or die. It had to find new lands and peoples to exploit and despoil, more raw materials to turn into wealth. There must be no turning back, they shouted, waving the flag.

In the nineteenth century, the Cotton Kingdom sought suzerainty over a slave imperium it dreamed of imposing on a wide area that would, by necessity, eventually stretch from the United States to Brazil. With the use of Whitney's cotton gin at harvest, slave labor cultivation produced enormous wealth for the planters. And as slave labor broke and ruined men, women, and children, industrial cotton cultivation exhausted and impoverished soils, and the cry arose for more land in territories and new states to be slave land and not free.

There were slaves in New Hampshire, at least for a while. In Warner on the war monument, with the names of soldiers from the town who fought in the Revolution, the War of 1812, the Civil War, and the Spanish-American War, is the name of Icabod Twilight, a freed slave, who—along with many, many African Americans, especially from New England—fought in George Washington's army.

The school myth is that President Harry Truman integrated the U.S. Army after World War II. But George Washington's army by necessity was an integrated army. As a consequence of African American valor and Washington's recognition of military necessity—he needed the men—black and white Americans fought side by side. Icabod Twilight was one of them. After the war Twilight's son, Alexander, graduated from Middlebury College in Vermont and became the first African American graduate of a four-year college, and the first to be elected to a state legislature. There's still a Twilight Hall at Middlebury.

African America valor and accomplishment made the horror and absurdity of slavery in a "free" nation all too apparent. Slavery was not only a chain around the necks of its victims but also one that ensnared the republic in its venomous pittfalls. Unfortunately, neither heroism by African Americans nor immortal words of freedom penned by slave masters like Thomas Jefferson could overcome the racism and the economic benefit for some that maintained the slave system in the land of the free and the home of the brave.

In the nineteenth century, the Cotton Kingdom established relationships with mill owners, both domestic and foreign, who turned cotton into fabric and then into finished goods and into their wealth. The mills of Manchester, New Hampshire, on the Merrimack River, and of Manchester, England, used U.S. slave cotton that ultimately provided about 90 percent of the world's supply. And the power of the empire of slavery was sufficient to protect the "rights" of slavers, through tortuous compromise after compromise with free states.

In the twenty-first century, the Empire of Oil identified its health with that of civilization, even as it became clear that information, not polluting, extractive industries, represented the future and profits of twenty-first-century capitalism. Software, entertainment, and finance were manifest in early twenty-first century corporations like Microsoft, Disney, and Citicorp as an expression of future prospects, not the depredations of the infamous Exxon-Mobil and its political retainers.

And, as in the nineteenth century, when the mill owners split with the planters, and the alliance between them disintegrated along with the Whig Party, it became clear as a matter of self-interest that the alliance between the corporations of the Information Age and the Empire of Oil was under stress. Fault lines widened with the entry into the political sphere—with their millions—of men like the storied twenty-first-century financier George Soros, who first attempted to play a crucial role against Bush the Younger in the 2004 election, and whose efforts proved decisive in later elections.

The now largely forgotten careers of two scoundrels, or perhaps near tragic figures, of our past exemplify the similar fate of the empires of slavery and of oil, and the genesis of a coming ecological turn.

Howell Cobb of Georgia was the incarnation of the cotton planter and the political face of slavery. Vice-president Dick Cheney was the most outspoken champion of the Empire of Oil. Their careers, separated by more than 150 years, reflect the common bonds forged between the business and political imperatives of the empires of their time.

Howell Cobb was a larger-than-life figure. He was the picture of the Southern grandee slaver. Civil War diarist Mary Chestnut wrote about Cobb as an actor playing Romeo in a stage production for planter friends. And she remembers Cobb, who wrote a book on the biblical justification for slavery, asking his personal servant with some emotion, "Whether I am to wait on you or you on me?"

Such questions of master and slave and their respective places under the Southern sun were important for Cobb, who owned 1,000 slaves, a million dollars in human property, on his Georgia plantations. He became a politician, was elected to Congress, and then was chosen to be Speaker of the House of Representatives, in a compromise, as a moderate slaver. Cobb became governor of Georgia, and he led the unionist forces against the early secessionists, who he accurately believed threatened continuation of the slavers' way of life. He was Secretary of the Treasury in the Buchanan Administration before the election of Lincoln, which led him to resign and join the secessionists.

Howell Cobb was a candidate for president of the Confederacy, but withdrew as Jefferson Davis emerged as a compromise choice. He swore Davis in as president, and was speaker of the Confederate house. During the war he served without great distinction as a politically appointed Georgia militia general. As Lee, in desperation, called for freedom for slaves who joined the beleaguered Confederate armies, Cobb was among the holdouts; insisting: "If slaves make good soldiers our whole theory of slavery is wrong."

Sherman burnt Cobb's plantation, sparing just the slave quarters. At the end of the war, Cobb was arrested, lost his slaves and much of his fortune, and died of a heart attack in the Waldorf Astoria in New York City.

Cobb's rise and then fall parallels the career of Richard Cheney from aggressive go-getter in Washington for President Richard Nixon and for Don Rumsfeld, to secretary of defense under President Bush the Elder, to conservative Wyoming congressman, to Haliburton president, and finally vice-president of the United States and intellectual leader of the failed presidency of

George Bush the Younger. Cheney, more than any other man, was held to be responsible for the paradigmatic Iraq resource war for oil and the relentless policies of the Bush administration that privileged oil and the growth of fossil fuel energy industries above peace, good sense, and ecological survival.

Cheney viewed energy efficiency and conservation as personal qualities, not as guides to public policy. He could find no line separating the interests of the oil industry from those of the United States. Like Cobb, Cheney viewed the world through a monochromatic lens conditioned by the needs of the oil empire, much as Howell Cobb governed in accord with his perception of the needs of slavery and slavers and their betterment.

The equation they both followed was similar and ultimately simple. For Cobb, for the way of life of the Cotton Kingdom, wealth and power meant buying more land to buy more slaves to buy more land. . . . Whatever facilitated or supported such ends was the basis of good governance and justice. Whatever opposed or inhibited the unfettered growth and prosperity of this way of life was to be opposed at any and all costs.

For Cheney, for the way of life of the Empire of Oil, wealth and power meant to control more reserves, to produce more oil, to control more reserves. . . . Whatever facilitated such ends was his guide for public policy and patriotism. Whatever stood in its way was to him an un-American imposition upon freedom and prosperity.

Cheney and Cobb stand as solemn testaments to the power of self-interest and self-delusion. They both came to power on the basis of their supposed moderation and intelligence to balance less able and more extreme men. But both ultimately used their abilities to further causes that by their nature were irredeemably corrupt and evil and whose pursuit could and would lead only to self-destruction.

The great gray wave of history rolled on. It was about to engulf Dick Cheney's Empire of Oil and us as it did Howell Cobb's Cotton Kingdom. In the twenty-first century we needed to find a safe harbor of peace, democracy, and ecological sustainability. Or else.

Four Innovations

The defeat of the Empire of Oil, unlike the destruction of the Cotton Kingdom, did not require a bloody civil war. The crisis that deepened from 2020 to 2060 was conflict enough in the face of the all-too-apparent consequences of industrial abuse and industrial politics. This established the basis for dramatic and fundamental change, the emergence of the understanding of what to do, and how to do it.

We had the sometimes daunting democratic task of making means approach ends, balancing freedom and community, moving from an industrial to an ecological social order. Our challenge was to use the principles of our past to construct ecological democratic orders of the future.

This task cannot meaningfully be discussed apart from the exercise of the revolutionary spirit and ideals that informed the steps that moved an industrial society toward becoming an ecological civilization over a period of several generations. The why and how are intertwined and interrelated. We need to take the measure of the spirit as well as of the writs of the times. But for the purposes of clarity, I'll tease out what are now seen as the key organizational and policy steps that led us from the afflicted past to our conditional enlightened present.

And while they can and have been subject to learned economic, political, and philosophical discourse and analysis, they have shaped and in turn been shaped by the daily and most ordinary rhythms of our lives. An ecological civilization was not handed down from above but shaped by the lifeways of the millions in response to the imperatives of our times. The broad themes, so clear in retrospect, took their present form as a result of nearly a century of practice, adjustment, and modification in response to our behavior and the exercise of democracy.

It was not science and new devices that saved us. We have taken advantage of scientific development. But this was never the heart of the matter. At the core was democracy and the way we used our democracy to enhance and reshape our pluralistic market economy. An ecological civilization and sustainability didn't roll off an assembly line or emerge from a laboratory. They were a consequence of our democracy.

Industrial wealth and power was, in many ways, also an artifact of democracy and freedom. An ecological civilization was a result of further democratic actions undertaken in response to some of the doleful and often unforeseen results of global industrial success. We had to change direction. And democracy could.

Four key social initiatives shaped how we shopped, how we worked, how we ate, the nature of our houses, our schools, our families, how we saved and invested, how we organized and governed ourselves, and where we sent our complaints, and offered our loyalties.

These four twenty-first-century initiatives have matured to become the twenty-second century's now familiar Four Elements of Sustainability and Prosperity:

1. An ecological tax system replaced *all* federal taxes on income, with two ecological consumption taxes on pollution, depletion, and ecological damage: an ecological value-added tax (VAT) and a British thermal unit (BTU) tax on energy. (April 15 used to be remembered not as the start of the baseball season but as a date of dread when federal income taxes were due.)
2. A national trust savings and investment system was established, funded by annual government savings, that invests strategically in communities to support sustainable jobs and prosperity. (These American Trust Bonds have become the most familiar and traditional gifts at important birthdays and family rites of passage, reflecting the timeless stability of an ecological system that has actually only been around for 100 years.)
3. A negative income tax ended poverty and welfare by lifting the poorest above the poverty line, and working families toward the middle class and a liveable wage, in exchange for fulfilling a responsibility for national service on the part of all Americans. (What we now take for granted as the time of service of our youth and a lifelong sense of security was, paradoxically, an early and formative creation of the ecological age, an idea that was pilloried by its industrial opponents for

allegedly limiting people's growth and future prospects.)

4. A plan was developed for our democratic continental American Union that reflected the transformation and expansion of the nineteenth- and twentieth-century nation-state to meet the challenges of a twenty-first-century world. (In a world of nations and of 17 continental and sub-continental unions, it's stunning to realize that less than a century ago we lived in a world of often warring states with their own armies and narrow sense of self-interest and governments that were as often dictatorial as democratic.)

The grand themes knitted together and are expressed though our now ordinary lives in Warner. The great dematerialization of culture that began in the twenty-first century has left us with relatively fewer of the things that filled the lives of the people who accurately and sadly called consumers in the twentieth and twenty-first centuries. We are today, of course, citizens and think of ourselves as such, not as purchaser of an ever-accelerating inventory of disposable products destructive of the earth and of human happiness.

We buy food at the Warner Cooperative Market; all of it is normal food-that is, in twenty-first-century terms, organic food—and much of it is locally produced by our own farms and greenhouses. Eco-taxes made the long-distance production and transport of food viable only at luxury prices for luxury items. Similarly, much of the plastic crazes of the twenty-first-century oil culture have given way to sustainably produced paper and fabric packaging.

Plastics fell dramatically out of fashion not just as a result of soaring petrochemical prices but also when it became clear that the leaching of minuscule amounts of estrogen-like chemicals from the plastics into food and water was responsible for both a dramatic decline in human sperm counts, health, and motility, leaving a large percentage of men effectively sterile and leading to many fetuses being prone to spontaneous abortion and neural system birth defects. And, as plastics fell from grace, where paper and fabric weren't sufficient, nanotech production from organic feedstocks filled the bill.

In 2144 we pay most of our taxes through the ecological value-added tax (EVAT) when we buy things. The more polluting, depleting, or ecologically damaging the product, the higher the tax. It hits you in the pocketbook, before you decide to buy. The market lets you know. Since most things are now sustainably rated, we usually pay a flat 20 percent tax. But for the real baddies, the tax rate can soar to 500–1,000 percent. You can still buy an internal combustion engine vehicle burning biomass-derived fuels, but who'd want to spend 200,000 instead of 20,000 on a zero-emission hydrogen-electric vehicle, unless you're a very rich and dedicated eccentric or hobbyist.

The Warner General Store, an affiliate of Edmund's, which has run a hardware and general store in Henniker for centuries, now sells the usual range of durable catalog goods. When you need the unusual, they can usually produce what you want from the nanotech information synthesizer. The stuff's not cheap, but it doesn't wear out, at least not before you do, and is fabricated using sustainably rated materials. And when things are worn out, they become future feedstock for the synthesizers or are composted as organics and spread on the farms as fertilizer or used in the gardens.

Informatics and information are, of course, big business and the stuff of global net commerce, as well as pleasure, communication, entertainment, art, scholarship, education, politics, and governance. Exchanging, trading, distributing, buying and selling information, experience and knowledge is the foundation of the global economy and the source of much of Warner's income. Significant trade-offs have been made sacrificing speed for sensuousness and completeness in cyber-experience.

In many ways, in our twenty-second century, the power of the global network, combining informatics with simulation technologies tying the world together in a historically unprecedented fashion, makes us more rather than less local. Our emulations can sit and talk comfortably around conference tables at meetings gathering representatives from any number of continental unions. We can look one another in the eye while we are sitting in our living rooms.

We have manifested, in an increasingly elaborate fashion, the global village foreseen by the informatics prophet Marshall McLuhan in the twentieth century. The power and sophistication of the unseen data side of the global net allows us to communicate using the seven basic sense channels of sight, sound, smell, touch, taste, temperature, spatial orientation. These, of course, can be conveyed on the basis of actual conditions, simulated, compiled, or chosen as consensus reality.

It would be more than a little distracting for representatives from 12 unions at a meeting to experience 12 different meeting places simultaneously. These could be compiled into a kaleidoscope of sensation where a place is both hot and cold, bright and dark, fragrant and foul. . . . So it makes more sense to simply agree that we'll meet at my house or gather in my garden and have that be our common experience, forsaking for the time being almost all others, beyond our need to be warned or become aware of changes in our immediate environment that requires our attention. Alternatively, we can decide to get together in a simulated room, or grotto, or seaside.

Of course, simulation cannot compete with the real thing in an ecological world. But the sensory data channels have made possible interactive remote contact. Lovers across the world can meet together in an agreed-upon place and experience each other's real touch, taste and smell as their emulations come together. They can also experience, if they choose, enhanced synesthesia, giving color a sound or sight or a fragrance. The experience is artificial, but it is based on real intimacy and feeling, not a simulacrum of that. Love trumps pretense.

And as the poet asked:

> Can love prevail when
> passion becomes duty unlimited
> ignorant of time and space?

These are not just issues for philosophers. Love, which demands limitless connection, has always taught, as a consequence, restraint. That is never so clear as in the twenty-second century, when the necessity for making those choices has often arisen. What is the guilt and the burden attached to net infidelity and physical intimacy between emulations of people separated by oceans? Can there be really good marriages between lovers who have never met in person and are passionate, intimate, and faithful yet have made love only through emulations?

As a reality-monger I have my own opinions. I have to admit that the smiles and the joy on the faces of the beloved in their emulated sanctuaries give me pause. I had thought that there was a bright line between reality and emulation, no matter how good and interactive and suffused with real-time sensation and experience the emulations are. It's really the smell of your hair and your breath right now I am sensing. But still that's at a digitized remove, at second hand, no matter how accurate and complete, grasped, sensed, and experienced through our emulations.

The emotional connection and emotional reality between real people brought together through informatics is undeniable. The unavoidable tendency is to suggest that such interactive experience at a remove has crossed or at least straddles the line, and that willing and direct experience over the net is within the broad ambit of lived emotional reality. Not my choice for a way of life. But a way nonetheless.

I must admit that the opportunity to swim along the now largely fully recovered Great Barrier Reef, to taste the salt water, feel it rushing over my skin, see the myriad brightly colored fish nosing up to me for a look and the flash of a Great White in the distance, also curious, when I've fully booted in, does have its place. How much does it matter here if this is taking place through real-time sensory input from the reef or complied, complete, and no-to-mention affordable emulation?

Really making love in the grass with your sweetheart has no comparison. To do so across the continent when separated by circumstance is second best. But the opportunity to embrace Helen of Troy or Hector, depending on your preference, in a grotto outside the walls of Troy is also an interesting experience.

And, of course, simulacrum science has long learned that the "giveaway" of informatics, what made it different from the real, was its unadulterated perfection. So successful compositors began to add the further spice of flaws and the unexpected, changing the "E" or emulation nature of the once-perfect fantasy moments. To fully appreciate a good time, you had to have the experience of being rejected by your fantasy woman, who could meet your every need reliably, endlessly, falsely. For then she was in spirit similar to an old blowup doll sex toy, or an exercise in pornography where the gasping and desire is endless, but unreal.

Balance. Balance was the great discovery of the ecological turn. Industrial man and industrial woman too easily became lost in the world of excess that absorbed lives and life energies in the ceaseless quest for more that filled their days, robbing people of their peace and their leisure. The great balancing cry of *Enough!* gave us the time and restorable human energies to be able to join fullheartedly in doing a day's work, playing, and making love and also enjoying, if you choose to, an excursion to Troy.

The rising of balance to a central place in a world of now nearly infinite options over the global net was a logical consequence by necessity embracing the moderating and balancing moral sense and teachings of people like Rabbi Hillel, Aristotle and Diogenes the Stoic to help us follow a sustainable middle way. Industrialism made it all too clear that unlimited want leads to catastrophic excess. Ecological civilization understood that the enormous powers and consequences of its means needed to converge with sustainable ends.

A Visit to the City

Cities have always been the glories, the signatures, and the shame of civilizations. Sustainability has over the generations changed the twenty-second-century city. The overwhelming impression, I believe, would be that less is more if you somehow could step from Boston at the beginning of the twenty-first-century to Boston today, in the middle of the twenty-second.

Boston in 2144 is quieter, cleaner, safer, and greener. There are fewer people, fewer vehicles, and far less pollution. On the other hand, there are more people in the streets at all hours, more urban farmers today than stockbrokers. More sidewalk cafes.

From Warner, the trip south resembles more that of the railroad era of the early twentieth century, when Warner had seven stops on the Boston & Maine Railroad and tourists from the city came north in search of the earliest ski slopes. The auto journey over the interstate highways 89 and 93 has become a memory of the Age of Pollution.

The mag-lev system stop is once again along the Warner River, two miles away down Newmarket Road, where the Boston & Maine feeder line ran north toward Sunapee. Now the stop is on a branch that carries you at high speed and without fanfare to the city, with its excellent transport system, mixing ubiquitous mag-lev jitneys and, of course, the various types of Segway transporters, from the Personal Minimals to the Family Jitney.

The social innovation of sustainability was to let Boston be Boston and Warner be Warner. Communities did not just move from auto traffic to packed mag-levs, whose speed could have permitted commuting over greater distances into the city and encouraged more early twenty first century–style anonymous suburban and edge city growth. Instead, twenty-second-century development is decentralized; mag-lev capacity is strictly limited. The lesson of the twentieth and twenty-first centuries was *If you build it, they will come*. This was for better and very often for worse. Less sometimes really is more. We visit the city. We work near where we live. The means of transportation in the twenty-second century have improved. The need for twenty-first-century-style commuting has radically diminished.

Warner's identity as a producer village was enhanced, and Boston's city nature and character flowered. Over the generations the neighborhood character of the city was strengthened and enhanced through the creation of superblocks, generally using as borders the old main avenues, which still had car and truck traffic. Within the superblocks, new town squares and pedestrian malls were formed from the land reclaimed from cars. An increasingly pedestrian world flowered.

The city superblocks have become self-contained and self-interested urban nuclei, each with a particular social, artistic and economic character: neighborhoods within neighborhoods. Within these superblocks grew our own Boston versions of dynamic souks and medinas, shaped by local custom and character. As in the traditional city, neighborhoods became places substantially inaccessible to quick auto entry, reachable in general on foot (or Segway).

Bridges for pedestrians and Minimals spanned the avenues connecting superblocks. The avenues became mag-lev transit corridors and truck delivery routes. In Boston in 2144, most people pick up the kind of Segway they need at mag-lev stops and pay either a yearly subscription or charge day-user fee.

As soon as the city turned its back on the car and its insufferable arrogance and demand for instant accessibility, human character and diversity flowered. Astounding cultural energy was expressed, from the new art districts to the new flower markets suddenly manifested through local initiative. Freedom and community in motion is an astounding force for renewal.

Clusters of superblocks represented and heightened the character of neighborhoods. Southie was the seat of the Boston Irish Renaissance. The South End was a haven and entrepreneurial center for Boston's Asian diaspora. The North End, in the minds of many residents, rivaled Milan for the dynamism of its fashion industry.

Because of the removal of the impediments of the auto and of urban ultrapollution, cities became a place of protean creativity and entrepreneurship. The community business focused on the superblock, and the neighborhood plan was in its way similar to small-town Warner. By its nature, the city fostered the growth of co-ops of co-ops to form large organizations and enterprises capable of cooperative action in support of one another and of appropriate scale and resources to take advantage of opportunities.

In many ways, the neighborhood and the superblock created their own markets. And the second- and third-degree groupings of co-ops and community-based businesses provided enterprises with sophisticated planning research and sophisticated managerial and financial resources that hitherto had been the province only of large corporations but were now focused on and controlled by communities.

A new class of urban farmer arose, growing food on land reclaimed from the auto, given over to green space and safe from pollution. The farmers cast their plots, as well, across rooftops and along transport median strips. The economics of their operations was supported by the EVAT system that favored local production. It stopped making economic sense to move perishable food around the globe instead of producing it on the next block.

The Boston metropolitan area, of course, has emerged as the Union's education mecca, with Harvard, MIT, Boston University, Boston College, Northeastern University, Tufts University, and Emerson College collaborating on the great global data preservation and accessibility project. This coordinated the new global open source, open access transparency of the net, to make each node of the global network, in practice, as capable as any other and capable of sharing in the global information bounty.

The rise of the information age was expressed in conception and sense of identity as a library where information was available to be used by all, and where discovery was shared, as opposed to the bank model, where information is treated as wealth to be withheld and guarded against encroachment.

The city in the twenty-second century became a place not where people wielded power and accumulated wealth but a venue where diversity was given the opportunity to flower and to create.

Boston, like Warner, was a place where people were again drawn to the beauty of the river. And on a Sunday along the Charles, filed with sailboats, many scores of men and women could be seen in the riverside parks carrying or setting up easels to paint their interpretations of this urban glory.

Ecological Taxation

Of the four innovations shaping the twenty-second century, the first is the ecological tax system. We tax pollution, depletion, and ecological damage, not income. We abolished all taxes on income. Instead we are taxing all consumption of both goods and services on the basis of how polluting, depleting, and ecologically damaging they are. The more polluting, damaging, or depleting, the higher the price.

Market forces through the price system send ecological signals along with the trillions of daily purchase and sales decisions. The ecological tax system levies taxes before the fact. This makes us think before we buy. Prices are directly related to the degree of pollution, resource depletion, and ecological damage caused by the product or service.

We tax the bads and not the goods. By getting the prices closer to right, the market sends signals for sustainability. *Buy cheap, save the planet*, as every school kids knows

What initially seems the impossibly boring and dauntingly complex stuff of tax policy on closer examination is neither. We've developed a system in which the immediate self-interest of lower prices is largely congruent with the general interest. Of course, this does not mean we are automatically home free, or that this market is all-wise and self-regulating. Rather, we have created a social market system where the market rules cause market signals to approximate social and general benefit.

Over a decade's time in the twenty-first century, income taxes were gradually abolished as the new ecological consumption taxes were phased in. For each dollar raised by ecological taxation, there was a dollar drop in income taxes.

When income tax freedom day occurred after a decade, a great sigh of relief rose to the welkin, and April 15 is still celebrated as Income Tax Freedom Day. It's our most lighthearted holiday, dedicated to a celebration of foolishness, a goodhearted national Mardi Gras. My favorite is the selection of Tax Freedom Day kings and queens, in the old English tradition of the wise truth-telling fool, to remind us with humor of things we had rather not face the rest of the year.

At first, in the twenty-first century there was a BTU tax on energy that raised as much money as the EVAT. In the poison power epoch, fossil fuels and nuclear power predominated. Like the EVAT, the more polluting, depleting, and ecologically damaging, the higher the BTU tax. This made sense, since energy was the major source of pollution before the Renewable Revolution.

Once poisoned power had to charge the true costs of production and use, the Renewable Revolution began in earnest. Renewable resources were quickly adopted. They were not just better; they really were cheaper. Renewables swiftly becoming an important part of the energy mix, then the norm, then the standard, and finally predominant.

Renewable resources were cheaper, decentralized, ecologically friendly, and a boon to employment, self-reliance, and sustainable prosperity. Zero emission in vehicles, mass transit, power generation, heating and cooling, and manufacturing meant that cities were dramatically cleaner, quieter, and safer. The skies became natural blue or grey. Urban agriculture on rooftops and in backyards and the new median plots became an important new food source and occupation.

From the standpoint of taxation and sustainable transformation, the BTU tax no longer made sense as renewables became predominant. There was no longer any meaningful amount of fossil fuels to tax, no significant amount of gasoline pouring like a river into the gas tanks of cars and then, as polluting exhaust, belching into the air. The BTU tax was folded into the EVAT, and everything was subject to the single ecological tax.

Zero pollution became the watchword, not just of ecologists, radicals, and dreamers but also of the Harvard Business School. The paradigmatic moment was Harvard Case Study 2079-43, about the production and investment decisions of BR, or British Renewables, once known as BP, or British Petroleum.

Generations of B-School students begin their training with examination of this case and its updated corollaries in the introductory courses in finance, production methods, and taxation. As the B-school teaches, "Business ethics is sustainable business" and "Sustainability is the way to maximize present and future value." By 2085, students often took a joint masters at Harvard from the Divinity and Business Schools, which are now both part of the Harvard Center for Sustainability whose dean, by tradition, holds the Harvey Cox Chair in Sustainability and Ethics.

In our time, *business* and *ethics* are no longer an oxymoron. "Business is fun!" according to the latest campaign to attract students to business schools and lighten the sense of seriousness and gravitas that has adhered to the profession, where to be called a polluter in 2140 is similar to being called a Benedict Arnold in Revolutionary times.

The marketing mavens quickly made the differences between high- and low-taxed goods and services quite clear. At first, six colored labels, from bright green to green to blue to red to grey to black, told the story of relative tax rates, ranging from zero to punitive rates for items still legal but enormously taxed.

Of course now price, tax, and product information dances before your eyes with a wave of your hand, as the resident product chips sense moving human infrared, or at a distance, if you're holding a shopping wand or wearing a shopping bracelet or sporting data goggles. Data accoutrements or not, the colored label told you instantly much of what you needed to know at a glance.

Bright green:	Zero tax	
Dark green:	Lower tax	(.5 x average tax)
Blue:	Average tax	
Red:	Above average tax	(1.5 x average tax)
Grey:	High tax	(4.0 x average tax
Black:	Highest tax	(8.0 x average tax)

If the average EVAT rate was 25 percent for an item priced at 100 Americans, a blue label would mean you'd pay 125 Americans; a black label would set you back 300 Americans.

Beyond the label, early twenty-first-century computers could handle the data side of the ecological consumption tax transformation easily. First it was electronic barcodes on products to be read by scanners, providing information on the product's sustainability ranking to determine the tax rate. Then it was information that became part of the ubiquitous cheap smart chips resident on almost everything sold. The chips were read by your E-communicator and cash registers, although precious little cash was still used, and the information was also accessible on the net as part of the informatics revolution.

For the accountants and technoids among us, the EVAT started with ranking the amount of pollution, depletion, and ecological damage of each industry by their three-digit standard industrial classification (SIC code). As time went on, the same was done with progressively smaller subsets of the industrial galaxy until finally it became product specific. And new SIC codes were established as needed, for example, to account for renewable energy resources and organic agriculture and nanotech.

And while critics forecast an enormous bureaucracy would be set up to wrestle with determining the taxes on a myriad of items for sale, reality proved much simpler. Determining tax rates by broad SIC code was not that hard to do. Effects being clear enough and gross enough for an industry on average, if anyone took time to look, although there certainly were surprises. To depart from the industry tax average and gain lower taxation, it became the responsibility of manufacturers to present data to prove that their product or service was in fact less polluting, depleting, or damaging.

Warner Industries, for example, made sure that its nanotech inputs and outputs were both fully reusable, nontoxic, and organic to win a presumptive pollution and depletion green rating for its outputs and lower taxation. But, of course, it mattered what those outputs were. A nontoxic earth-raping device—an earth-sterilizing toxic sprayer, like a "safe "nuclear weapon (meaning one that would explode only when it was supposed to) was clearly not the road to sustainability or, in our case, to a lower tax rate for the degree of ecological damage.

Some activities that seemed innocuous turned out not to be. Large-scale concrete production, for instance, proved, in practice, to be an inordinate producer of greenhouse gases and responsible for much habitat degradation through enormous material flows and the disposal of overburden and waste. Therefore, this activity became subject to high tax rates. Nobody builds houses on traditional concrete slabs anymore. It costs too much.

The underlying strength of the pollution tax system is, of course, that it has a positively reinforcing effect on progressively reducing pollution. This proved to be the most significant feature of ecological taxation.

High taxes put the worse polluters out of business. To maintain tax revenue, what had been only moderately polluting now carried the highest taxes. The E-tax system simply uses the mechanism of the market. This is not moral but economic jujitsu. High prices on polluting, depleting, and ecologically damaging items suppress demand. Entrepreneurial energies produces lower prices and less polluting, depleting, and ecologically damaging alternatives. At the same time, E-tax rates increase to maintain revenue on what used to be medium polluting products and services, which now are the most injurious in the aggregate.

The systems dynamics go on and on, forcing out high-polluting items and moving ever closer to an almost flat tax in a low-polluting world. Over time, as the overwhelming number of goods and services came to be within the sustainability band, those that we judged outside this band were enormously taxed and were swiftly impelled by economic forces to change their ways.

The average EVAT tax rate of 25 percent was sufficient to raise most of the twelve trillion in constant Americans needed for the annual American Union budget. The American replaced the dollar much as the Euro became the common European Union currency.

From the time of economist Judy Elliott's pathbreaking book *The Ecological Rebirth of the Invisible Hand*, it became clear that *comprehensive* ecological consumption taxation had resolved the problem of targeted ecological taxation of eliminating by its success the sources of revenue.

The early ecological tax efforts were aimed at identified sources of pollution. For example, crude oil and polluting products and sinks were taxed, and the economy was allowed otherwise to function under a typically diverse and complex income tax regime. The theory was that eliminating the sources and sinks of pollution and the revenue that targeted ecological taxation raised was what we were looking for.

The problem with conventional targeted ecological taxation was threefold. First, it misunderstood the extent to which sustainability was a question not just of pollution and depletion but of conduct and habitat destruction and ecological damage that resulted from the most allegedly scrupulous means.

Second, it underestimated the extent to which production and consumption decisions at all levels were suffused with sustainability issues that could not be effectively captured by taxes on material inputs and outputs. Sustainability is a matter, at bottom, of consequences and effects that often have to do with scale and questions of social ecology, as well as aggregate matters of fossil fuel use.

Third, there was always the problem of adjustment of ecological taxes to reflect dynamically changing processes, technology, and production and consumption decisions. A comprehensive ecological consumption tax system is concerned not with inputs and outputs but with aggregate effects of *practice*. The targeted ecological tax system encouraged the use of new and exotic processes whose consequences had not been accessed. The struggle then was over the prerogative of the gatekeeper to allow or disallow the use of new products and processes. And if new processes were allowed, the battle would start all over again when and if they were to be taxed.

And while the adoption of the precautionary principle was a major victory in the battle for sustainability, the advantages of a comprehensive ecological tax system became clear. All new products and processes would automatically be subject to the average tax rate for their process or product type, and then would be specifically tax rated. A chlorinated hydrocarbon product would, by its nature, be given a black rating (8 times the average tax rate). It would then be decidedly in the interest of the manufacturer to demonstrate that the product would be licensed only to be used in ecological production processes with zero releases, in order to obtain a reduced tax rate.

The most frightening thing about twentieth- and twenty-first-century industrial pollution was that it was, in large measure, entirely legal and in compliance with copious environmental protection standards and laws and approved by the Environmental Protection Agency. It was not the work of polluters operating under cover of darkness. The largest polluters were, by and large, legal emitters and poisoners. Our greatest corporations were our greatest polluters. And our government was the single greatest polluter of all. How things have changed.

The twentieth-century industrial system taxed income after the fact, generally without regard to its ecological consequences. Income tax systems encourage externalities, the socialization of the cost of pollution. Under an industrial income tax and regulatory system, pollution was overwhelmingly a public cost, while profit remained private. The incentive was to pollute, keep the profits, and hire lawyers and lobbyists and buy politicians to keep the unfettered profits and pollution flowing.

For nearly 100 years, the coal-fired Bow Power Plant on the Merrimack River, owned by the Public Service Company of New Hampshire, cast a stream of legal sulfurous mercury and particulate-filled gas over the countryside. The plume from the plant, usually blowing northeast with thc prevailing winds, was clearly visible from Interstate Highway 89 heading south from Warner, as you drove in your fume-spewing, gasoline-powered, internal-combustion-engine car on the way to the state capital in Concord, 5 miles north of the plant.

The plant was in compliance. So was your car. Hard as that is to understand today. So was the Seabrook nuclear plant, spewing radionuclides into the air and generating a stream of short-lived and long-lived radioactive wastes. The dome of the plant today is encased in a further mantle of concrete and steel, its inventory of high-level radioactive fuel rods stored in concrete sarcophagi, as a consequence of just a few decades of poisoning, arrogance, and plain stupidity. It will remain where it is as a monument to industrial crimes against the biosphere for tens of thousands of years into the future, while the plutonium in the fuel rods slowly decays.

Legal. It was mostly all legal and the province of captains of industry, ribbon-cutting politicians, leading scientists, our greatest corporations and financiers. Such was the march of industrial folly. Much of the force of law and universities and organized religion was mobilized to provide justification for the industrial juggernaut and its insatiable conduct, identified as the best of all possible worlds.

Industrial growth was the *summum bonum*, the highest good, to be measured in the dollar value of the economic activity, whether this was the cost of cancer care, coffins, bombs and bullets, or decontamination and waste storage. It was all good. It was *more*. It was a reflection of ceaseless and, by definition, inexhaustible industrial economic dynamism.

Its mad genius was the capture of human freedom and human reason, enlisted to serve industrial ends. All was possible within the province of *more*. You could invent, build, market, sell, as long as it meant ever more. You had a perfect grant of freedom to attempt to continue to spin the industrial wheel faster and faster.

Again, Thoreau's speculators, who spent their days buying and selling the forest to be cut for lumber and pulp, were valued infinitely more than the man, woman, or child who passed the time wandering through those woods wondering, leaving only footprints and taking just ideas.

It was anointed as common sense, the everyday procedure of a great global industrial empire that owned and controlled the present and mortgaged the future. But, of course, like all exercises in arrogance, profligacy, greed, and stupidity, that empire undermined and destroyed itself and nearly all of humanity and much of the living world. Left are the sad monuments like Seabrook, the industrial dead zones in various states of slow recuperation, and a deep democratic commitment that we cannot follow that path again.

In those days, regulation worked with an income tax system to declare certain amounts of pollution acceptable and legal. They would require constraint only when they rose to the level of regulatory concern. This system gave rise to refinements such as "cap and trade," whereby regulators, with the connivance of lobbyists and politicians, set limits of levels of pollution that would slowly decline over time, and conferred rights to pollute on the poisoners who could sell poison entitlements to others needing to poison more or not to take steps to reduce pollution.

The effect of such programs was to institutionalize pollution at levels considered acceptable by the poisoners in the name of efficiency and jobs, but largely for the sake of maximum profit and not in the interest of sustainability or health.

Over time it became all too apparent that for the market system to be able to continue it was absolutely necessary to eliminate rather then institutionalize poison. The ecological tax system was developed as our best response to enlist the power of the market in the cause of sustainability, democracy, and prosperity—all gravely threatened by industrial excess. This was excess that led to all sorts of desperate calls for the necessity to abolish or "reform" markets through dictatorship and command, in the interest of saving what was left of the planet.

It seemed, for a while and for many, that the clearest and, in fact, the only way to respond to industrial excess was to order it stopped. Those who believed in the power of the strong state, supported by various strands of neo-fascist and neo-Marxist ideologies, offered prescriptions for a grey future.

Fortunately, that was not to be, and our democracy crafted a better way, preserving both the freedom and the community upon which it relied. Democracy in the end proved to be the only effective choice. Who else could solve our problems for us?

Trust for Sustainability

The second social innovation shaping the twenty-second century has been the American Trust for Sustainability. The trust invests, by law, between 5 and 10 percent of our tax dollars every year in sustainable projects to support the growth of sustainable jobs and sustainable communities. While the ecological tax system sets new social market rules, the American Trust focuses social investment in sustainability and primes the pump for change.

The underlying principle is sustainability through investment in community and cooperative entrepreneurship, in an economy shaped by ecological market rules and price signals.

The American Trust may sound like another grey and uninteresting institution. Why aren't I discoursing about the miracle of hydrogen catalysts and cold fusion devices developed at the Mallove Center and the solution to the energy problem? Scientific invention and technological change, in fact, was potentiated and conditioned by social innovations, in response to all-to-apparent necessities that arose in the crisis of the Age of Pollution.

It's worth noting, as we consider where we have been and where we are going—the primary motivation for this book—the common faults of both socialist and capitalist industrial prophets. Most obviously, they ignored the underlying dynamics of *industrialism* as a social practice that underlay the differing, but still basically similar, conduct of industrialism's capitalist and socialist manifestations.

A Karl Marx or a Milton Friedman focused more on the success of their industrial variant in competition with the despised alternative. The ownership and control of the industrial machine for them was the thing. They did not see that the nature of both would be conditioned by common industrial practices, in accord with and guided by the industrial ideology: the steel triangle of industrialism combining hierarchy, technology, and progress.

The American Trust was a way to use our tax money as savings and investment to respond creatively and constructively to the crisis of industrial civilization. Radical change can have everyday roots. The American Trust was such a radical departure. Instead of simply spending tax money on transfer programs or squandering it on weapons of war, or corporate subsidies, the American Trust invested and loaned money to catalyze sustainability and an ecological transformation as a feature of economic growth.

Under the ministrations of the American Trust, operating in accord with the opportunities established by the ecological market rules of the E-tax system, economic growth came to mean ecological improvement, not ecological destruction. In the twenty-first century, to do well meant you also needed to do good.

The American Trust invested in community-based businesses, in new sustainable industries, in moving existing businesses toward sustainability, in community facilities and institutions, in housing, in whatever made sense in local and regional development plans.

From the standpoint of Warner, the selectmen worked on a community sustainability plan and initiative as part of the master plan for the town that helped us decide what we wanted to become over time. It was not so much a prohibitive exercise like zoning as a facilitative exercise that helped town residents, businesses, and institutions obtain support from the American Trust whether or not they were officially town-managed or not. We are in microcosm a bit of the world network economy, communicating and connected to one another and offering mutual aid to one another, as we have been in this small New England town for more than 500 years.

As a formal organization, the Trust has regional development banks with elected boards, a national coordinator elected by the regional boards and confirmed by Congress, or the highest legislative body for each member nation of the American Union, and a small, Union-wide executive committee composed of the national coordinators and a support staff.

The Trust has two divisions, investment and development. Development works with communities and cooperatives to encourage the practice of social and community entrepreneurship. Its job is promotion and planning to help the community pursue sustainability through business investment.

It offers sophisticated planning and management tools to help with the formulation and implementation of sustainability plans for the community, state, region, nation, and beyond, as well as assisting with individual business enterprise plans to help accomplish sustainability goals. The Development Division plans.

The Investment Division is responsible for making decisions on how money is invested. It acts in accord with its fiduciary responsibility for the conduct of sustainability with its triple bottom lines—the ecological, economic, and social. It's an investment bank that represents a river of capital to help build sustainability firm by firm, region by region. It's an investment bank whose charge is to do good and do well.

In many ways, the American Trust is where the action is. Its Development Division planning and promotion departments work closely with local and regional cooperative banks. Its Investment Division often participates as a loan or equity partner in projects initiated by local banks and institutions. When the Warner Farmers Cooperative wanted to build the new organic feedstock plant, the Sugar River mutual bank turned to the American Trust for capital and planning support.

There were two basic consequences of annual American Trust capital increases in the range of 100 billion dollars a year from E-tax revenue. Trust resources were set by statute at 10 percent of loan portfolio, and this meant that each year almost an additional trillion dollars in new loans were to be made anywhere in the world. The American Trust was responsible both for enormous global investment for sustainability and at the same time generated enormous cash flows for the bank and further investments.

This income stream from equity or loan capital, with required returns being in the 6 percent range, meant a doubling of Trust assets in 12 years. By 2144 the Trust generated sufficient income to begin to replace a considerable amount of revenue raised by the E-tax system. It is expected, if sustainability investments allow the Trust to continue to double, that in the context of sustainability, it would be possible to actually abolish the E-tax system as a revenueraising measure.

Yes, an end to taxes through investment, peace, and sustainability. Perhaps the twenty-second century will prove Ben Franklin wrong about some things, and taxes, if not death, will prove ephemeral.

After a career as a sustainable development consultant, I was elected in my semi-retirement to the board of our regional development bank. By inclination, I'm not given to the deliberative and decision-making role of a board member. I'm much more an in-the-field guy, with my hands stuck in the dirt or designing and testing systems. But as a consequence of having made so many mistakes over the years, I was deemed in my semi-dotage to have become sort of wise. So I accepted the nomination. One of the unintended consequences of the more deliberative practice of Trust board service was this book. From a focus on yes or no, the question of why began to loom large in my mind.

The management principles informing the Trust are those of democracy and subsidiarity. Power and decision making rest to the maximum feasible extent with those most concerned with the decisions at hand.

That is, people in Warner make decisions about what's recommended to the Regional Trust Board, but regional decisions are made on the regional level. The Continental Board deals with the broadest, most general issues—how much money is needed, how in broadest terms should it be invested to assure sustainability in all its aspects-ecological, financial, economic, social, political. Within these broad guidelines, the national boards function, then the regional, and then the local.

Sugar River Bank is still on the corner of Kearsarge Mountain Road and Main Street. Since its early twentieth-century start, it's been a mutual bank owned by its depositors. After the Great Panic of 2052, almost all existing major financial institutions became insolvent. They emerged from bankruptcy largely as cooperatives, mutual banks, and community institutions in exchange for federal bailouts, with a commitment to sustainability.

The secret of the survival of the Sugar River Bank was the development over the decades of an ever-increasing amount of community-based and controlled capital earned by the new profit centers of the global network economy of the twenty-first and twenty-second centuries. Ownership was largely by co-ops, the new limited community corporations, community-owned enterprises, and community-based nonprofits and sole proprietorships. The American Trust would often have an equity share, most particularly in non-voting preferred stock, to help maximize and securitize trust income over time.

The American Trust worked hand in hand with the new ecological market rules and imperatives established by taxing pollution, depletion, and ecological damage. The new market rules opened the way for the development of new industries. The wind, solar, hydrogen, organic feedstock, and nano-syn industries and infrastructure grew, with the support of the American Trust, into a network of community-based complexes organized as needed into a variety of larger cooperative structures.

The American Trust not only prevented market failure by being willing to loan to new and community-based business, but also became the preeminent source of the *patient* capital that was necessary for the effective pursuit of sustainability.

The impatient fascination with quarterly profit results that speculators declare must ever increase was a major contributing factor in the destructive march of an unrepentant industrial capitalism.

The change to the patient practice of capital invested for sustainability was a more astonishing accomplishment than the new settlements on the moons of Jupiter and Saturn, the cities rising along with a reformed Mars atmosphere, and the mining of the moon for frozen water deposits to generate hydrogen, through solar photoelectrolysis, for both rocket and base fuel and oxygen.

Despoiling the solar system, they say and I agree, while we measure and *now* moderate every jot and tittle of our conduct in the interest of sustainability as a consequence of centuries of abuse. And, of course, it's claimed that development beyond the earth's atmosphere meets all international treaties and regulations and is conducted under the Sustainability Treaty that binds all Unions, in the name of all humanity, to the peaceful and sustainable use of space, spectrum, and celestial bodies both planetary and otherwise. But without almost any knowledge of the local context how can we justify imposing a human footprint on a pristine planet or moon? Yes, in theory it's degradable material. In theory.

But let's not kid ourselves. We're explorers. Conquistadors in our own right. And we're still waiting, and will be for 646 more years, for a reply from what we take to be a multiplanetary civilization in the Haroon System whose robust electronic output is screened by the enormous output from the Crab Nebulae that exists in front of it as a Niagara of blocking white noise across a very broad frequency spectrum. It was only the use of the coordinated computing power available on the entire global net that in its 143rd year, the Search for Extraterrestrial Intelligence (SETI) Project was able to discern regularity and meaning amid the noise.

After many debates about the reality of what the SETI scientists became sure they were hearing, and the wisdom of making a reply, it was decided to spend a major fraction of the exploration budget and send back a signal. To do this, a communications probe would be constructed and then launched from the moon base, with sufficient hydrogen fuel to accelerate into space at a 145-degree angle from the planetary orbital plane.

After attaining 45 percent of light speed and traveling for 7 years, the probe would be at an angle such that the signal would only be partially masked by space noise from the nebulae and would begin to send a series of reply codes—based first on intervals of 3.1417 corresponding to pi, and then switching to a series of prime numbers—to impart the unmistakable inference that an alleged intelligence, that is, our own, was at work answering back.

Skeptics cautioned for years that it might be better to keep listening and attempt to understand the messages before responding. They could be trading recipes of ways to cook humanoids, or providing orders of battle, or directing the search for new conquests. . . . The scientists figured that any civilization that had achieved so robust a communication spectrum would likely have transcended, by evidence of their survival, any earlier proclivities to inevitably self-destructive and self-limiting violence. We were putting ourselves in the position of a man grabbing a wolf by the ears to see what would happen and was now unable to let go . . .

We had enough trouble dealing with our own planetary system. Why invest so much time and effort to share the most slender benefits of humanity with a civilization as yet untouched? But after endless choruses about the human spirit, how we are not alone, and divine will, the Probe project sucked up many billions of capital, its subsidiary communications enterprises receiving funding from the American Trust. They were to explore the terrestrial and planetary possibilities of the new interstellar communications technology and that latest and greatest expression of a new branch of informatics: interstellar.

Like all tools, the American Trust is as wise as its wielders, and the benign intentions of its means cannot be separated from the consequences of its ends. So once again it was proven that good intentions and a fixation on grand schemes can and will lead us to experience unintended and sometimes malign consequences. But I'm just an aging reality-monger. Out of step, out of step. Out of leap, I say, that leap into familiar stupidity. The Probe is now an antenna in deep space, relying on the great bat wings that are both monitors of signals from Haroon and photovoltaic arrays to capture light in deep space to generate sufficient power to relay messages expected in response to our greetings.

Community ownership though the American Trust has indeed made us more secure and more patient. But not necessarily wiser. The Probe project is just one more example of spending money on technology and on things *out there* when the real action is and should be *here*. Enrich the sustainability of our lives here. Even build more museums if you have to. I can stand the often humorless exercises. The Museum of the American Hippie being the happy exception. But I'm just an old man, 96 years old, almost two-thirds of the way through my now expected seven score and ten, so my words can be put down as a confabulation of nostalgia, regret, and the dreams of an old man. An old man who did accept age enhancement and somatic gene therapy.

Since most of us, in the great rush toward sustainability, identified our own interests with those of the planet, the patience of the American Trust in the management of capital elided with the patience of an expected healthy 150-year life span and the absolute necessity for sustainable conduct in a world where we wanted to live longer and had to be willing to radically reshape the dynamics and consequences of human habitation on a fragile planet.

It wasn't childhood's end, and it isn't immortality. But it is a far more extensive period of dynamic, productive adulthood. It meant for us the embrace of new kinds of families, and of group parenting-raising single children with the insertion of common genetic material so that one child can look like, or at least resemble to some extent, all seven or eight parents.

The paradox of our brave new world is that by extending our life span we have also radically limited our conduct. We have smaller families, constrained appetites, and blinkered conduct, a more circular and less expansive relationship with one another and with the world. Such are the joys of sustainability. They are real. But they mark a change. There has been an ensemble of benefits. But there have also been a plethora of changes that our democracy has chosen and that we have embraced as individuals and that is shaping our lives in most profound ways. The most profound changes are ones that are so little noticed because they have become integral with our everyday existence.

The Negative Income Tax and National Service

The third social innovation shaping our century is the right to receive a negative income tax in exchange for meeting the responsibility for national service. The negative income tax (NIT) effectively abolished both poverty and welfare. It lifted the poorest above the poverty line and the working poor to a livable wage. It was a major part of the basis for an upward harmonization of the American Union, where a sustainable prosperity within bands of acceptable difference is shared by all.

In exchange for meeting the requirement of 24 months of national service, now Union service, every citizen has the lifetime right to receive the NIT, which provides for each of us basic existential security without the intrusive stigma of welfare. As a Union citizen who has met the requirements for service, one has the right to sufficient resources to live modestly but well. And isn't living modestly but well what sustainability is all about?

This isn't a paean to penury. It is an assertion, as Tom Paine argued in the eighteenth century, that each of us is entitled to a basic share of the public wealth as citizens that will enable us to lead productive and secure lives. The NIT is not based on punishing the rich. Rather it is an assertion that we all contribute and all of us in a democracy deserve the right to a basic share, recognizing that we all start with different endowments, both personal and material, that we have no control over and that are a reflection of past acts and circumstances.

Thus today a basic right of passage for youth is the period of service that is undertaken in a wide range of diverse ways appropriate to abilities either great or constrained. Service qualifies all of us to be able to live our lives with confidence that we will have our *basic* material needs satisfied. There's a sense of dignity and self-responsibility in knowing you met your basic service requirement. You may not be able to walk; nevertheless, you performed appropriate service.

Service for some has been working as umpire and groundskeeper for the

Kearsarge Mountain League at Govoni Field, named for Warner's major leaguer, Mark Govoni. He was an all-star shortstop for Florida, playing for both the Marlins and the Devil Rays in the 2010s. He's best remembered for the "Double Steals" in both seventh and the ninth innings of the 2014 series against the Red Sox. In the seventh he doubled and then stole third and home to tie the score, and in the ninth he walked, was sacrificed to second, stole third, and scored the winning run on a suicide squeeze where the bunt was missed for a strike and he slid in under the catcher's tag. Yet another Sox loss was Warner's gain. And they still don't know how to win. More accurately, they remain stylistic masters of the loss, to be redeemed only by a World Series triumph twice a century. It's good, say Sox fans, that we can now live long enough to see the Red Sox win two World Series.

Service for others has been working in the blueberry farm fields on Waldron Hill, pruning the bushes and building the organic compost system. Some people built houses with Habitat, Warner being a bicentennial Habitat community, where neighbors make sure everyone ultimately has a decent house in which to live.

Habitat has a loose alliance with Merrimack County Housing Cooperatives, a handler and wielder of equity and American Trust funding. Habitat never has done that, persisting for generations on volunteerism and spiritual mission, not institutionalized funding. Habitat instead relies on the conscience that informs our basic sense of justice and fairness, the sense that each of us has the right to a home informed by a duty to act to make sure that happens for everyone, even those few who still slip through the cracks in our community. That's freedom and community.

Volunteerism and mutual aid are the root basis for that spirit. It's what the Amish and Mennonites and the New Shakers have done and still do today. Cooperative housing is a manifestation of an ownership and entrepreneurial society that's built, in part, with our participation and labor. Union Service is part of the sustaining basis of that system.

The essence of Union Service is to find appropriate task or tasks for each young person to do, or create jobs that need to be done to enrich the lives of our community and the lives of our youth. It's part of gaining the majority in our century. It's voluntary. It has a series of compelling incentives through lifetime benefits. But it can be deferred or avoided altogether. And that's okay.

What the responsibility for national service and the accompanying lifetime right to receive the NIT has done has been to fundamentally transform expectations. Existential security is taken as a basic and earned right of Union citizenship. You've earned your right to live a modest life. As an active participant in our sustainable society, you are a participant in the ownership and control of social as well as personal and community property. You likely own your job, your home, your land, your school, and your hospital through some combination of property rights that are part personal, social, and community entitlements. And these property rights are backstopped by the NIT, which guarantees a basic income that moves the poorest out of poverty and almost all to a livable income.

Gone in this century are the old intrusive bureaucracies, with the stigma of welfare or the dole, by any euphemism. This was the path of punishment and monitoring for being poor, and of self-perpetuating failure and discrimination. If we have done one thing right, it's to recognize that education, personal initiative, and a balance of rights and responsibilities are the path toward dignity, existential security and, most crucially, sustainability. Without social justice, no sustainability, and certainly no peace.

Justice, it turns out, is a matter not of charity but fundamental self-interest and collective benefit. The NIT established the basis for sustainability as social practice. It removed the goad of poverty that allowed the imposition by necessity of exploitative conduct by the rich upon the poor and their acquiescence in the destruction of the living world. There's a quite different debate that goes on between the hungry and the well-fed, compared with discussions among the universally well nourished.

The NIT is also experienced within the context of a commitment to free lifelong education and training. Education and training are free. The NIT allows people to meet basic needs while pursuing education and training. The income from the American Trust was directed first toward the NIT, social insurance, and education and training.

The NIT has given us time to consider. And time is one of the fundamental characteristics of sustainability. Industrial time is always *now*, as part of the demand for *more*.

The NIT changed the equation between time, work, and wanting. The NIT gradually encouraged the pursuit of other personal and social goals than maximizing. Sustainability is an edifice we have built based on the principle of *enough*, in contrast to an insatiable industrial demand for still more.

Continental Unions of Nations

The fourth basic social innovation that has given shape to our twenty-second-century world is the continental union of nations.

This was a necessary increase in scale and complexity to help resolve the seemingly intractable problems of the twenty-first century when nation-states had neither the power to limit the depredations of war and ecological destruction, nor the ability to take effective and corrective action to build a sustainable world. The nineteenth-, twentieth-, and twenty-first-century world of competitive and often warring nation-states has become a world of largely cooperative democratic unions of nations on a continental scale that encompasses 93 percent of the world's peoples and has relationships with most of the rest.

Today there is, of course, our American Union, the European Union, which stretches to the Pacific since it includes Russia, the Near Eastern Union, which extends from Morocco and Tunisia in northern Africa to Israel and Palestine and to Iran, the Sub-Continental Union of India, Pakistan, Bangladesh, and Sri Lanka, the Asian Union, the Pacific Union, the African Union, the Southern Pacific Union, and the Polar Union. In addition, a number of smaller subunion groupings associated with the Union system, like the Asian Mountain Alliance of Nepal, Bhutan, and Tibet, which maintains ancient traditions outside the union model.

What was necessary in response to the all-too-apparent agonies of the Age of Pollution was democratic organization on a scale and complexity sufficient to successfully reshape our imagination in response to changed circumstances and help enable us to act effectively and creatively to resolve our problems.

There was a conversion of global interests in the wake of the then astonishing successes of China's leadership with its "The East Is Green" initiatives in the 2070s, 2080s, and 2090s. China, by then the world's leading economic power, was moved by necessity to creatively and fundamentally restructure its relationship with its Asian neighbors. China used and successfully adapted the by-then-venerable European Union model in the interest of ecological sustainability and global coordination.

Paradoxically, it was easier for the Chinese to take this step away from the nation-state. China was both the ascendant economic and political power and, at the same time, the conscious embodiment of several millennia of continuous Chinese cultural and national identity that had preceded the existence of the Chinese nation-state. The global leader, by relaxing some of its narrow prerogatives, was also expanding its influence and rising *cultural hegemony* that was not measured in military or narrowly political means. Chinese leadership had been able to develop under the shadow of the United States' once global military dominance, which effectively relieved China of the pursuit of the folly of military competition and an arms race with the United States with its global imperium and ultimately nearly completely self-destructive military hubris.

In China, the one-party state gradually became an active democracy over the decades. It became clear that the costs—social, political, economic, and cultural—of the maintenance of a tottering dictatorial bureaucracy were simply too great and served as a hindrance to Chinese national self-assertion and leadership. The United States regrettably failed, in its long reign as global hegemon, to successfully respond to the all-too-apparent need to adapt to the gathering global ecological, economic, and political crises that industrialism had wrought.

The Chinese, perhaps ultimately because of their cultural maturity, were able to accept the new mandate of heaven and exert leadership toward the effective global growth of ecological unions. But it may also be argued that what happened was largely a question of circumstance. It could be said that the United States' turn toward the Green was sincere and energetic, but was handicapped by the legacy of too many years of an industrial dominance that had transformed what had been American leadership into the mere pursuit of the grudging obedience of vassals, so that America's world leadership was sacrificed on the altar of resource wars and greed.

The United States' twenty-first-century view of a zero-sum world with winners and losers proved to be a self-fulfilling prophecy. While the U.S.

empire was the loser, the American nation was decidedly not a casualty. The passing of global leadership to an ecological Asian Union led by China, with the powerful participation of the entire retinue of Asian energies of Japan, Korea, Taiwan, Vietnam, Thailand and Indonesia facilitated a new American renaissance.

Freed from the shackles of imperial pretension, a Jeffersonian nation reemerged, admired for its freedom and community and creative energy, much as the original American nation of the Founders had been a beacon of hope 350 years before. *Live free or die* really meant something again. What mattered now was not the reports of victory or defeat from American armies around the world but what we did and how we lived *here*, in the spirit of the philosopher Albert Camus, as neither victim nor executioner.

Chinese leadership helped set the stage, demonstrating what was both necessary and possible and facilitating action. And while the geopolitics of the decades of recovery after the Troubles of the mid-twenty-first century informed the growth of our ecological and democratic unions, it is also true that the continental-union arose from below, as a logical extension of vital community and of self-management, democracy, and mutual aid writ large.

Unions were not imposed from above upon a conquered populace and cowed nation-states. This lack of coercion was certainly true for the American Union. Rather, the continental-union system gradually flowered as an expression of largely cooperative initiatives from below. It was clear that the time of the nation-state was passing. Much as the red flag had once been struck from the Kremlin with little fanfare and little violence as the old Soviet empire crumbled of its own weight in the late twentieth century, the maintenance of the prerogatives of the capitalist industrial nation-state became too much to sustain.

The Union system freed nations and their communities from the limits and costs imposed upon them by states and was a logical expression of the coevolving global network economy, society, and culture.

From the standpoint of Warner, we are not staring up at the commanding heights of power. Rather, the feeling is that the instrumentalities and the power of the state have moved farther *away* from us. Brasilia, São Paulo, and the Union seem very distant across a darkling plain.

The Union does its job. But much of that job involves the machinations of the Union Congress, which, by and large, these days are considered harmless. Their role is very much to clarify and coordinate, as necessary, national initiatives that are deemed to be applicable as Union-scale policies within the framework of national differences and democratic participation.

The most significant evidence of the Union in our lives is the operation of the Union Trust, whose investments are increasingly displacing Union taxation. Administration is decidedly both national and regional, acting in accord with very broad guidance, adopted—with our participation—at the Union level.

Community enterprises, community nonprofits, and cooperatives that are organized into networks undertake most social functions. The Union has little to do directly—outside of Union Trust financial investment—in areas ranging from police, education, and housing to health care. The model of organization is closer to a radically democratic version of the classic private transnational corporation of the twenty-first century. The nations are largely independent and self-managing entities. The Union facilitates communication and cooperation, codifies and adopts standards and policies proposed from below, pays attention to infrastructure and coordination.

The Union does not wield a heavy managerial hand or control a huge bureaucracy. Rather, it represents a small, highly networked, data-gathering, and coordinating staff that serves the democratic decisions taken by consensus of the Union Parliament on most matters, or by voting when consensus is not obtained and a decision is deemed to be an operational necessity according to the Union Constitution.

So, from the standpoint of Warner, the Union appears to be small and far away, and like the wise Chinese emperor and follower of the Tao, governs with a sure but very light hand indeed.

All the Unions are different. All have certain basic things in common. First, they are democratic unions of *nations* that have ceded some of the prerogatives of states to the union. Nations in 2144, in general, don't have armies; they have national police. National armies were abandoned in favor of police, while the union possessed powerful, albeit limited, defensive military forces. Nations use Union currency. Nations are rooted in the Union economic and social order and are active parts of the global network economy and society.

Nations retain aspects of their traditional identity and territorial boundaries. They have and maintain customs in common that from the standpoint of outsiders are illogical. Like *Live free or die*.

These national frontiers are unguarded frontiers. As Union citizens, we all have basic rights and responsibilities that include the ability to live and work where we will within the Union. Freedom of movement for people was an even more difficult question to resolve than questions raised by the freedom of movement for capital.

These questions were resolved over time, in substantial part, as a consequence of the pursuit of justice and fairness for all within the Union. The pursuit of justice made where you live a matter more of freedom than desperation. In 2144 almost all of us have a basic sense of existential security. This is manifest most particularly by the Union Trust and the negative income tax. We are not hungry. We are not hopeless. We are not destitute.

Unlike the workers of the Industrial Age, we have escaped the treadmill of endless work to feed endless wants. We've traded, in large measure, the material for the immaterial. This does not mean that the material has automatically been replaced by the spiritual. But our sense of well-being and satisfaction is rather at a remove from what we have bought. It is more focused on what we have done. The consumptive fevers of the twentieth and twenty-first centuries abated, by necessity, in the time of the Troubles. But positive reinforcement, resulting in the rise of play, leisure, and pleasure, has been infinitely more significant in shaping the embrace of sustainable ways.

We went from the *See the U.S.A. in Your Chevrolet* twentieth-century equation of purchase with efficacy and pleasure, to the injunction to see the U.S.A. through a virtual tour, mag-lev glider, or city scooter as much more a matter of taste, not the cost of acquisition. The focus became not what to buy, but what we could avoid buying.

In Warner, we generally live as we have always aspired to most of the time over the centuries—modestly but well. We have not banished ostentation or greed. But the underpinnings of sustainability within the context of strong community and the global network economy have led most of us in our lifeways to converge more or less near that golden middle. And for those who seek to trade leisure and play for accumulation and labor, so be it.

Existential security means that hopelessness, hunger, and poverty is not the lot of Union citizens. We have the expectation of a lifelong ability to obtain education and training. Health care is a fundamental part of what it means to be a Union citizen.

We are a dynamic and not a torpid society. But in large measure we work *with* instead of working *for*. Over the decades, sustainability and our increasing life span has meant that as the hours of work have decreased, the number of years of work have increased.

Union-affirmed rights and responsibilities do not limit nations in their pursuit of freedom, community and ecology. Rather, they set a common floor. We have abolished neither inequality nor wealth. But we have at least kept poverty effectively at bay. Spiritual poverty is more open to debate. But who can argue with happy days and lovers rapturously walking through the summer fields down to the Warner River to picnic and passionately embrace.

Conditionally we have accomplished what was the wan hope of the tie-died banners exhibited in the Museum of the American Hippie. We made love and not war. That central preoccupation of the nation-state, war, began to fade with the growth of democracies, and has been successfully contained in our century within and among the system of continental unions.

Democracies don't make war on one another. They are inherently inclined by their political nature, at least in regard to one another, toward notions of practical justice and fairness accomplished through political accommodation and negotiation. Not war. Industrial nation-states have made war with impunity upon undemocratic nation-states, as the all -to-bloody history of the nineteenth, twentieth and the first half of the twenty-first centuries makes all too clear.

The United States, as the world's leading democracy, was also the world's leading war-maker and militarized nation-state, with armies and global influence on a scale that even exceeded that of Rome in its heyday. By the early decades of the twenty-first century, it became clear that an endless war against terror had become a contest for the control first of oil, then of water, and then of food and agricultural land in the resource wars of the Age of Pollution.

It was a contest between the rich and powerful industrialized states of the North, typically democracies and the leading polluters and users, and the poor and often undemocratic nation-states of the South, whose role was provider of inputs to the global industrial machine under the suzerainty of the Empire of Oil.

The industrial nation-state system was preeminently a war system and a pollution system where power and the recourse to war and the threats of war against the poor were common currency. This was facilitated by the dictatorial client regimes that were fostered and maintained in these exploited states. With democracy, the powerful states' ability to wage war and to impose their will dramatically declined, along with the rapid depletion of oil resources and the rapid development of the global climatic crisis.

The Union is not the traditional state writ large. Rather, the war-making proclivities of the nation-state have been obviated, both by the growth of democracy as a near universal, and by the removal of war making powers and armies from the nation.

The individual states of America became potential member nations of the American Union, free to identify themselves as parts of additional national and subnational groupings. New Hampshire, Vermont, Maine and Atlantic Canada are proud members of the Nor'east Nation, with National Assembly, common and cooperative plans, and a relationship with the Union Trust as a national group.

The United States of America, of course, still exists as a nation whose member states share and celebrate a common historical, cultural, and economic heritage. But the U.S., instead of a global super power or military levithan, has become largely a means for states to extend mutual aid and cooperate in areas of common interest.

Today, nations within their unions are not just territorial,but also a self-defining means of identification and community. In New Hampshire and in Warner, Franco-Americans identify themselves with the nation of Quebec and often participate in some common social insurance, cultural, and business activities, much as Lutherans still participate in common investment and retirement plans.

The principle behind the democratic unions is the encouragement of a maximum amount of voluntary agreements, relationships, and interconnections. Trade and contact are the watchwords. We've become a culture more of workers, burghers, farmers and fishers than of soldiers.

The war psychosis, wrapped in militarism and patriotism, that identified national feeling with blood and war, mass armies and mass killings was calmed through the growth of Unions and democracy as a fundamental Union practice. Fortunately for humanity, mature democracies, and certainly sustainable democracies, are never at war with one another. Conflict within and among unions is and has been resolved by other means than war.

We have certainly not ended all violence or conflict. Riots erupt. While officially we have no slums, and poverty, by definition, no longer exists in the American Union and its nations as a consequence of the Negative Income Tax (NIT) and the Union Trust, we are not perfect. The Army of the Urban Poor (TAUP) waged a campaign first of nonviolent noncooperation to demand justice and real opportunity from Boston to Santiago. Cries of half-measures and co-optation splintered the TAUP and led to the violent resistance known as the new terrorism in scattered cities.

For a time five years ago, it was considered dangerous for outsiders to venture onto the Boston Common. The TAUP uprisings were resolved finally through a blanket offer of amnesty, combined with the efforts of the new Union Organization for Democracy and Justice for empowerment and mitigation strategies.

And there are still occasionally racial and ethnic disputes where blood is spilled. Unscrupulous politicians and the powerful still, on occasion, attempt to exploit tensions and historical antipathies between black and white, Sunni and Shia, gay and straight, Christian and Jew. This is the violence of the blood feud and of the tribe.

This is violence exploited by demagogues to stay in power and avoid change. It cannot be eliminated, but it can and has been contained, its energies channeled into competitive sports like ultraball, and moderated by social mediation within the contexts of the Universal Union Commitments to Justice and Fairness.

While we have not escaped violence, the American Union murder rate is now under 100 per year, and this includes a number of economic crimes that led to deaths. And global statistics typically show less than 1,000 traditional murders annually.

Within the Global Union system, we have escaped war as an organized and endemic feature of human social and political organization. The Global Unions are now mature democracies. And democracies do not make war on one another. It wasn't as easy as passing resolutions, or worse, imposing resolutions on nations, that say *You're all democrats now.*

Sustainability meant the active pursuit of peace and justice as essential concomitants of our coevolution from an industrial war state system to a world of ecological democracies at peace. Sustainability means more than our market rules that punish pollution, depletion and ecological destruction. The democratic union system was built on the embrace of justice as inseparable from peace and from ecological sustainability.

The interests of rich and poor converged in a global system of nations that made it an essential act in the pursuit of freedom and community for the rich to constrain their short-term appetites and to help the poor move successfully from desperation to thoughtful democratic decisions. The twenty-first-century world of a few score billionaires and several billions of the impoverished was the apotheosis of the industrial death system, founded on essential injustice that potentiated misery, violence, repression, and instability.

The system of democratic continental unions arose as a necessary level of social complexity writ large—of sufficient scale and diversity to both effectively limit and redirect the conduct of an industrial civilization toward the ecological, and to encourage the flowering on a global scale of self-management in a global network economy and culture.

While a defining characteristic of the nation-state was a monopoly on the sanctioned use of force and violence, and an unspoken endorsement of the necessity of its use, the Union system rests on the embrace of democracy and self-management. Self-managing democracy as a world union system did not mean the application of a heavy hand by a well-ordered and carefully managed world-governing system. Rather, it was the flowering of our old New Hampshire ethos writ large, *Live free or die*.

People from away weren't much needed to tell us what to do and how to do it. We were and are quite capable of taking care of our own business, thank you. The Union established the basic ecological market and justice rules and the infrastructure that encouraged the maximum ability to form relationships, contacts, and agreements.

The provision of services, for example, fire and rescue, or schools, or police, could be by government, by volunteers with government support, by co-ops and socially sanctioned cooperative agreements, or by contract. We live in a universe of democratic organizations not all of which are governmental in which we have a vote and a voice. Soldier is still a profession, but the real activity of the Union military force is largely in response to needs for ecological restoration, disaster relief, and mediation.

There are still segments of humanity in certain areas that have not embraced democracy and joined the Union system either, in defense of custom and tribal tradition or within what remains in native reserves. It is within the tribal areas and their occasional wars that Union defense forces are sometimes called upon by the United Nations Council of Unions to serve as peacekeeping forces. And, of course, there are still even raids on Union territories from such redoubts as Baluchistan and occasional threats that amount to high-level blackmail to use weapons forbidden under the Global WMD treaty of 2074 by criminal enterprises masquerading as nationalists.

Twenty-eight years ago, the designer toxic chemical attack on the American Union administrative capital of São Paulo killed over 7,000 people before it was successfully antidoted. But this horror and outrage was largely a threat made good to enforce a high-level shakedown, and the Pirate-Tong-Mafia axis found itself faced by such global revulsion that its money could buy it no more safe havens; within three years, its leaders were all captured, and it ceased to function as other than marginal and local criminal enterprises.

Violence has been conditioned by the democratic practice of justice and fairness and thus sustainability writ large. As much as I'd like to claim that the scourge of violence has passed, I cannot. Violence remains a shadow—contained, rare, but still endemic, waiting, like the plague germs of Albert Camus's fascism in old chests and dusty bookcases, until they can again rouse their rats for the affliction and education of a happy city.

This is not a perfect world, in aspiration or reality. The four social innovations: ecological taxation, the Union Trust, the negative income tax, and the continental unions have helped us build the dynamic of sustainability as living practice. It is not perfect. It is what we have and an expression of what we have become.

Industrialism to Ecological Civilization: An Examination of Principles

I realize I've been writing much about what we know, how we live, about nuts and bolts and the reasons why. That's all well and good.

But it's also necessary at this point to take a step back and attempt to engage some of the philosophical implications of the ecological turn away from industrialism. This stepping back will help us gain perspective and perhaps help us to understand what has happened and to artfully change directions where we must.

So, with your permission, I'd like to spend some time examining the sinews of the extinct industrial beast and consider aspects and dynamics of its ecological successor. This may not be for everybody, but I'd be remiss in not providing ways to help us appreciate the qualitative and not simply quantitative nature of our civilization that rests on the everyday maintenance of ecological sustainability. We need to be able to understand how we have come to this point, where sustainability is the ordinary and usual course of affairs, from what was once a world ruled by the common sense of the self-destructive industrial leviathan. Sustainability will not take care of itself. It's up to us and to the choices we make every day. The more informed our choices, the more likely we will be to craft creative solutions to difficulties forseen and unforeseen that lie ahead.

Industrialism's Steel Triangle: Hierarchy, Technique, and Progress

Industrialism as a way of life rested first on hierarchy, a belief in order and command and the wielding of power as the basis of social order. A few people, mostly men with the authority of ancient patriarchs, ascended to dizzying heights of power over enormous economic and political structures.

And, as good hierarchs, their desire, above all else, was for power and profit, and for *more*. In industrial terms, this meant more production and consumption, its maximization without limit. More was measured variously in capitalism and socialism. But whether translated into monetary profits and power for capitalists or surplus output and power for commissars, the end was the same, poison-belching smokestacks, and piles of product for consumption without end. This was product for domestic use or for war both as an expression of *more* in the contest for power.

Hierarchy had at its beck-and-call technique—science and technology and bureaucracy—put to industrial ends. Technique was the tool that industrialism's masters and slaves used to hammer the living world into the shape of industrial ends. Humanity and nature were to be subdued. Marx sagely noted of the practice he observed of capitalist industrialism (socialist industrialism did not yet exist): "All that is solid melts into air."

The very mountains could be leveled, the fields paved, the farmers driven to become workers in the cities, millennial and sustainable ways of life summarily destroyed to meet industrial ends in response to the soulless dynamics of an industrial world. Industrial appetites are endless. Science and technology were therefore given the opportunity to channel all aspects of human creativity to serve the industrial master. Bureaucracy, empowered by telecommunications and then the computer, put technology to work in its malign service to manage and coordinate global production, consumption, and war schemes. Meanwhile, laboratories disgorged new processes and products, new ways of transforming and consuming the earth's substance, in accord with the industrial demand for *more*, ever *more*.

This was twentieth-century ecological prophet Lewis Mumford's megamachine in action. In response, he raised such simple and prescient questions as "What law of nature has singled out the increased application of energy as the law of organic existence? The answer is: No such law exists . . . any excessive concentration of energy, even for seemingly valid purposes, must be closely scrutinized, and often rejected as a threat to ecological equilibrium. The notion that the megamachine is in fact omnipotent and irresistible came in . . . with the cult of Divine Kingship: the primal myth of the machine."

Even after the collapse in the late twentieth century of the United States' socialist industrial rival, national laboratories continued to develop ever more innovative and devastating weapons and killing machines. This was done initially in the name of a war against terror launched by the oil empire in order to secure its dominance as the crises of depletion approached.

As oil reached its Hulbert peak and production irrevocably declined globally in the early decades of the twenty-first century, the great crisis began, with its economic, ecological, political, and military aspects. For a while, there was a desperate search for technological fixes to keep the industrial machine and the power of the oil empire intact. But the world of industrialism was falling apart, along with the Empire of Oil and the prerogatives of the United States.

And this end of industrial ways, as we know, proved to be inevitable, and ultimately welcome. There was no turning back, and the way forward was conditioned more by our four social innovations than by the gee-whiz solutions issuing forth from laboratories. Technique, in thrall to industrial hierarchy, would always produce new marvels to meet industrial ends. The issue was then and is now, what are we trying to accomplish, and for what purpose, and for whose benefit?

Industrialism had an ever-ready answer to the question why: *Progress*. Progress was a cult that justified industrial ends and changes needed for or resulting from industrial growth as both inevitable and the highest good. "You can't stop progress," people would say as the Town Forest was cut, farms paved, the interstate highway routed almost through downtown Warner on the west side of the Warner River. One of the old town cemeteries is left to languish in the median strip of the interstate. Like the Abenaki whose culture the settlers trampled and displaced, the industrial machine consumed, transformed, and devoured its way through the nineteenth, the twentieth, and the first part of the twenty-first centuries with impunity.

Healing Responses?

But human freedom and community and human reason itself could only be kept for so long in thrall to the machine. Excess would call forth its countervailing and healing responses. The largely nonviolent and restorative ecological revolution, rooted in new social inventions and innovations, would help us revive freedom and community as a vital center for our lives and help save the day.

That excess leads to a countervailing and ultimately healing response is one of the two great themes of human social revolution—the dialectic—humanity's ability to respond dynamically and creatively to excess of any kind. This is not the dialectic of the eschatological prophets, of Marx and his followers in the nineteenth and twentieth centuries, that posited the rhythms of history leading to an industrial socialist end of history. This proved to be no truer than the capitalist's great and glorious capitalist market nirvana that the scarcely bridled pursuit of profit would bring.

Overlooked by industrial socialist and capitalist prophets of supposedly fated happy endings, was the action of that second and more often neglected dynamic informing human social evolution, a tendency toward an increase in complexity and often scale in response to persistent social problems that have resisted resolution and threatened dire consequences. Sometimes the healing response to excess involves not just another way, but a way that's grander and more complex.

Such an increase in complexity is often seen as just another example of progress when viewed through an industrial lens. But, in fact, it is often not just the case of the same but more. An increase in complexity can represent a fundamental break with the past, a qualitative and not just quantitative change.

The movement from an industrial world of often warring nation-states competing in a capitalist market became, over the decades, an ecological world organized into a global network economy of nations who were members of democratic continental unions. The difficulties of industrialism could not be resolved by a return to earlier and simpler ways, although these certainly inform our conduct. A world of 9 billion needed over time to become a world of four billion living sustainably. But the tools for that decrease over generations needed to be chosen through freedom and community. The alternatives were an intensification of the wars, famine, pestilence, and mass migrations that afflicted the world in the twenty-first-century time of troubles and would have led, if unchecked, not to a happy landing, but to the end of civilization and the possible extinction of human beings, joining the hundreds of thousands of species that had perished as a consequence of industrial excess.

Newton-Ladd's organic orchard on the top of Gould Hill, which has been in the family for 12 generations, rediscovered and adapted nineteenth-century organic fruit-growing techniques for the twenty-first-century environment. Patriarch Doug Newton didn't have a choice. He couldn't afford to buy the oil-based chemical fertilizers and more successfully use the increasingly toxic pesticides and fungicides against now-resistant species.

The frighteningly irresponsible industrial genetic engineering practices of inserting biological toxins into the fruit genome also proved to quickly breed highly resistant superpests. It was, as well, prohibitively expensive to purchase designer gene rootstock. This would mean uprooting your whole orchard to start from scratch with supposedly pest-proof stock and discovering, once the trees were mature, that the pests were already well on their way to resistance. So it was back to the old ways, and communicating over the web to other struggling farmers, organic by necessity, what worked and what didn't and why.

The consequences of the ecological revolution were to some extent the use of updated older and simpler ways. But this was within the context of a much more complex and diverse and interactive global economic and political world. The amount of trade and communications by 2210 had increased by several orders of magnitude from early twenty-firstcentury levels.

Trade, it is true, is now largely in information, not material goods, and much production is now local and customized, using the latest nanotech devices and sixth-generation CAD/CAM production systems linked to the global production database. Much of what is still moved long distances are materials not available locally, primarily for reuse, and occasionally virgin, for things that still cannot be reused as inputs or feedstock for other purposes or recycled.

Our simple life rests upon an exquisitely complex industrial ecology; sophisticated ecological technological systems; a web of global interconnections over the net; a dynamic local political, economic, and social system that is based on democracy, participation, and local control, but rooted in larger democratic political, economic, and social structures of hemispheric reach and indeed often global scope. "So simple it's global," as the popular saying goes.

Socialist and capitalist industrial ideologues not only confused a transformative increase in complexity with industrial progress, not only missed the time scale of change, but also confused industrial vectors of progress, measured by *more*, with the subtler and in fact more realistic measures of enduring sustainability. In the face of agony, revolutionaries want and need immediate change. Keynes famously said, addressing those who counseled that eventually this too will pass, "In the long run we are all dead."

But, by necessity, epochal change is the product of many generations; it takes time to penetrate all aspects of society and life; it takes time to consolidate its triumph, to change what passes for human common sense, to become the basis for the similar yet endlessly varied human lifeways within the broad theme.

Marx was wary of predicting what would happen after the revolution, aware that he could observe only the broad streams of human historical development that he believed flowed in only one direction to a fated end. But his politics and his party sacrificed democracy, and with it freedom and community, in pursuit of ends that were to be revolutionary and industrial—the administration of things for human benefit. The results were not unexpected, a dictatorship that became the suffocating unitary hierarchy of a one-party industrial state using its enormous power for industrial ends at the expense of freedom, community, and the living world, in competition with the capitalist leviathan.

Capitalism would prevail in the competition with socialist industrialism. It permitted multiple and competing hierarchies within the capitalist context, including a civil society that would eventually transform its nature. Capitalism's triumph over the communist foe was short-lived. The consequences of capitalist industrial conduct, more or less democratic or not, would become all too apparent by the mid-twenty-first century. Communism, as the most rigid industrial order, merely was the first to collapse, a half-century or so before its industrial capitalist variant.

And as capitalism crumbled, an ecological world rose to replace the industrial one. It is a world shaped by our social market, with ecological market rules, our democratic continental union of nations, and our international localism.

The Rise of Ecological Civilization and an International Localism

While the ecological tax system crafted market rules that would incline market decisions to be made in the interest of sustainability, markets never have been and never will be perfect instruments operating for the common good. Markets fail under the best of circumstances, since the lives of people and their communities are influenced by many factors that have nothing at all to do with economic rationality and a market's rules. This is true whether markets are termed capitalist, socialist, social, cooperative, community, free, or managed.

Market rules don't by themselves take account of discrimination or of even such a small difference in existing conditions (as cosmological theory now conclusively demonstrates) as was responsible for the development and differential dispersion of now-existing galaxies.

Our market is today called on a global scale a "social" market, which, as more than one wag has pointed out, is a kind of weasel word applicable more to college fraternities and sororities than our economic market system. In any case, all markets, by definition, are social. Over the years, the designation "social market" stuck as the least objectionable compromise term for the global activity of one type of market system that, in truth, has elements of all the others.

There is the strong cooperative and community-based sector that is now the predominant form of both ownership and the locus for market activity. But capitalist firms still exist, although within the context of social and ecological market rules. Most firms, including corporations large and small, became cooperatives over the years. But the *Monitor*, our area newspaper, for example, is still a family owned and closely held corporation, with both a worker and a reader representative on the board. The *Monitor* led the nation in the use of edible newsprint. "Eat your words," is still on the masthead.

Our market is undoubtedly free, both in terms of choice for producers and consumers, and in that firms can certainly fail and go out of business as a result of market forces alone. There's still no endless free lunch, although the term "reemployment" has replaced "unemployment." There is a rather seamless web combining such the negative income tax benefits for people whose firms fail, the Lifetime Education and Retraining Act, the transfer of positions among cooperative, community-based, and even capitalist firms in response to the now minor economic downturns, moderated by cooperative and community economic dynamics.

"Human capital is too valuable to waste" was the mantra of twenty-first-century community economic development guru Michael Swack that finally became the managerial standard. Nowadays, workers, by and large, also are owners, as well as managers, in the smart network. Workers are not just producers. They are profit centers. Now, firms discard workers, their human capital, with as much reluctance as they dispose of monetary capital. Instead of layoffs, workers can be intelligently transferred or "loaned" between associated enterprises in response to economic necessity and opportunity.

For workers, responsibilities go hand in hand with rights. "They pretend to pay us and we pretend to work" and "You get paid here as much for marching as you do for fighting" are familiar refrains from the industrial age of workers under the thumb of the boss. Now almost all workers are owners, whether as a cooperator, partner, sole proprietor, participant-owner, stockholder.

In principle, owner-workers have a real and direct stake in the result of their activities. And, in principle, workers in today's firms will benefit on the basis of their own work. The old-time stock market bonanzas are gone. Once upon a time, entrepreneurs would "take a firm public," selling stock and raking in millions, or even billions, for their ownership shares that amounted to a claim on the future income and efforts of the company's workers. This was the model of the old capitalist's industrial economy of boom and bust, speculation, winners and losers, wealth and poverty.

The American Trust and the New Exchange Market replaced stock speculation with debt investments that would be repaid on the basis of the profits or surpluses generated by the firm. This was a source of income for investors but not a stairway to limitless wealth and power.

In the early twenty-first century, the richest 100 multibillionaires had more wealth than the world's three billion poorest people. The great crises of the twenty-first century and the Time of Troubles put an end to that.

Today there are still those who are considered rich and others who are poor. But the differential is much smaller. Within the American Union, the negative income tax has lifted the poorest above the poverty line and the once marginal to a livable income.

In Warner, the people living on Pumpkin Hill still are rich, and those on Chemical Lane still are of modest income. But Chemical Lane has not been a dumping ground for more than 150 years. And its residents have sufficient income to live a life no more likely to be cloaked in misery and unhappiness than their more materially comfortable neighbors.

Whether the difference in income between the poorest 20 percent of the population and the richest 20 percent is 3 to 1 or 10 to 1 makes less difference than that the *1* represents the opportunity for a good life as an active, participating citizen. There's much more to life than work and money. And it's a quite reasonable and indeed preferred choice by the majority, not just in Warner but in the American Union to live modestly, but well. It's a common and indeed normal choice to forego hours of work for hours of art, of hiking and fishing and crafting, of socializing and gardening, for being with our kids, and our elders, for visiting, talking, hanging out, playing music, watching the sky.

The industrial fashion and pernicious absorption was with work, with money, with buying things, with production and consumption. In our century we have reduced, and in some cases eliminated, the difference between work and play and art. But inevitably some tension still remains.

The big discovery, the common realization, was when the term *enough* replaced the demand for *more*. An Aristotelian mean replaced a Nietszchean ambition as our guide for action. By the end of the twenty-first century, people realized what they already knew but had forgotten in the drugged industrial madness. A need for more leisure did not mean more work; more peace did not mean more war. Gratification need not be endlessly postponed. Gratification meant an embrace of sufficiency and sustainability, not a ceaseless demand for more and more evermore. Pleasure was preferable to pain; love was more availing than hate.

Sustainability meant not only was there no need to quest for the self-destructive and meaningless *more*; it was a positive good to search for the sufficient *enough*. *Enough already!* and *Basta ya!* became the guide for happy times indeed. Happiness nowadays is not in spite of the way of the world. Happiness is, to a considerable extent, a consequence of the ways we are.

It isn't perfect. There are still thieves and even eco-criminals and the odd murder. Lovers still break up, and there are unhappy families. What's changed is the depth and breath of the pain, which has moderated along with our intemperate and inappropriate desires for the material at the expense of the living. "Where you end up is still largely a result of where you are going," as the sage Yogi Berra is reputed to have said. And he's still right.

This is the broader context of our social innovations and of the American Trust that was an instrument to help us take care of business in ways that met our human needs, to move from the industrial demand for ever *more* to the ecological world's need for *enough*. In retrospect it seems very simple; in fact, it is hard to believe that so much pleasure and benefit could come from so simple and so small a realization. But like many secrets from the Buddha's realization of the relationship between desire and pain, and the banker's discovery that you can lend depositors' money 10 times over and charge borrowers more than you pay depositors, supposedly simple things can have profound consequences.

The American Trust was designed to prime the pump to support the ecological transformation in conjunction with the new ecological market rules, to deal with market failure, and to accomplish desired social ends that transcend market rationality. It may, for example, have been economically rational for Warner to participate in a unified school district with centralized middle and high schools. It *may* have made sense economically to bus kids for an hour and a half from Warner to New London, the big population center, and it *may* have made sense to build one large rather than several small high schools and middle schools.

But it really made no social sense. Our kids are better educated, saner, happier, and in the end better and more creative people with better hearts if we keep schools with 200 kids close to home. It's clear that once organizations, schools, and workplaces involve over 500 or 600 people, they inevitably become subject to bureaucracy and the impersonal. Of course, for some kids who didn't fit in, it was a good thing to take advantage of opportunities to go elsewhere that the charter school movement symbolized, as counterpoint to the return to the neighborhood school.

The 200 kids can, and often do, now go to classes through emulation both locally and with groups of kids anywhere in the world served by the network, which means almost everywhere. This can mean spending a day or a term in a school, for example, in Africa in the village with our palm wine producer friend's kids. History and cultural studies are taught by being there through emulation. There's nothing like learning about India by walking though the streets of Delhi, visiting a village in Uttar Pradesh and getting soaked in the monsoon.

Cultural studies. Ah, "cultural studies." I must admit euphemisms never become extinct. They just morph. "History" and "geography" I always thought were good enough. But *Relevance*, they said. Relevance for today's kids meant that geography became cultural studies. It sounded so much softer, kinder, engaged . . .

And, yes, an emulated walk isn't really being there. But it is a very good to excellent simulacrum of the experience. And the better it now gets, the more I worry about Sam netted in, wearing his sensory suit, spending time away—here but not here. That's been the concern of parents I suppose since television first appeared now more than 200 years ago in the 1930s with a six-inch black-and-white screen.

The latest net suit looks and acts very much like an enhanced kayaking thermal suit that conditions and transmits information and sensation. The clear goggles and mask offering sight and sound, smell and taste. But Sam's a good kid with a good heart, with real friends as well as net pals.

Going out to play for our kids sometimes means a run through the jungle without really leaving the house, and playing a net game can mean another heroic lugubrious slaughter of cave trolls in the apparently endlessly renewing Ring cycle, or a light saber battle along with Obe-Wan and Darth. Darth, that one-time avatar of the dark side, now for generations become a warrior for good against evil. I preferred the original, ancient villain. A friendly Darth is as appealing as the new production of Hamlet where the tragedy's bloody final consequences are instead resolved through discussion . . .

I digress. But digression and meditation on where we are, where we have come from, and where we are going is integral to this exercise. The present and our past are many things. But what they certainly are not is a smooth linear progression from then to now. Reality has been and always will be contingent on circumstance and choice, protean, and uncertain, always to an extent unpredictable and imponderable. In other words, it is real and alive.

This reality and vitality extends, of course, across all realms, from the material to the philosophical and theological. The ecological journey of humanity in our century has been in spite of, decidedly not as a result of, the industrial cult of progress.

Ecological philosophy and theology are not merely a sort of alchemy that turns doctrines of progress and supposed biblical injunctions to subdue the earth into doctrines of stewardship and the practice of a moral ecology where actions are to be judged by their consequences in all their aspects, not on the basis of ego and intent that too easily embraced all change as good.

The steel triangle of the industrial, forged from technique, hierarchy, and progress, became over the last 150 years the ecological circle. Industrialism's steel triangle is easily conceived as a framework of elements and a tool for action, a blueprint for construction of industrialism's pentagon of power. The ecological circle is more an oracle influenced by the principles of unity in diversity, the interconnection between experience and relationship, and the practice of a moral ecology. While a blueprint provides the most unambiguous of plans, the oracle is essentially ambiguous, dealing in prophecy, possibility, and prospect. A blueprint presents construction details; the oracle engages agency and fate.

I'm not *that* dew-eyed. We don't just consult the Pythia of the New Green Church. We have our scientists. Indeed, we have our scientists in plenitude, with doctorates arrayed in University bagatelles professing wholism, Gaean dynamics, applied catastrophics, biophilia, limitology, consequential limnology, the whole retinue of ecological sciences, with their manifestations, specialties and subspecialties, grand integrations and summations material, immaterial, and social.

Indeed, sometimes I recall fondly the wisdom of the Roman emperor Domitian, who banished philosophers from Rome. In our case it would be the scientists, who, like the philosophers of the first century, are often too pompous and too self-assured and contradictory pain-in-the-asses. But I digress. And as a kind of intellectual in New Hampshire and a heritage rural region to boot, I suppose I flatter myself by believing that my ideas are informed by a rural practicality and skepticism uncontaminated by the sometime foolishness of the academy.

I suppose I'm also asserting that because I still stick my hands in the soil and make organic compost, I'm licensed to theorize and opine on matters philosophical and ecological. And if you say I'm a fool, I can reply, no I'm a farmer, at least a gardener, and therefore able to do at least some things right and worthy of respect. Accepting that there is some positive correlation between practice and theory, I return to the ecological circle that has proved to be a quite useful means of orienting our ecological ways.

The ecological circle is formed, shaped and maintained by the three grand unities: between the one and the many, between experience and relationship, between action and consequences.

All in action leads us forward in accord with time's arrow. All in consequence lead us back in accord with response and moderation.

This meditation on action and consequence I expect was informed, at least kicked toward consciousness, by another glorious Thanksgiving Firehouse Wheel of Fortune turkey prize. Wager on where the spinning wheel stops and win a turkey. Meanwhile, drink whiskey, or what these days passes for it, from large pottery cups. And all of us coming gloriously together in the old firehouse on Main Street. Feeling so close together with our neighbors, feeling so well and finely stitched together, feeling the meanings manifest behind unity and diversity, the plurality of experience and relationship, and the moral ecology of action. Feeling the meanings strongly enough that I moved to set down my interpretations before they receded to the province of sentiment and myth.

Unity in diversity, experience and relationship, the practice of a moral ecology must be lived as well as thought.

Unity in diversity is the clarion call of ecology, and of coevolution. It is an expression of the balancing interplay between the one and the many, an expression of the dialectic of freedom and community. The whole is an expression of its parts. But it is more than the sum of its parts. The ecological worldview is the glory and the science of wholes as well as the cherishing and awareness of the singularity of parts. It is the poetic awareness of a John Donne, of no man as an island, writ large and common.

Experience and relationship as sensuous unity is the immediate context of an ecological world. We are not held at a remove from the world and other people. We are inseparably a part of it all. We act and are acted on. We live within a force field of feeling and emotion, of mutuality. The unity of experience and relationship is the brake on our common ecological experience and self-consciousness that helps free reason and human agency from the shackles of hierarchy, progress, and technique. Interdependency is central to our experience.

The practice of a moral ecology is the connection of action to consequences. This is mediated and potentiated by the melding of experience and relationship and the dynamic of unity in diversity. A moral ecology is manifest in the practice of mediation, dialogue, and equilibration of action and its aftermath. It is the art of weaving the web of life and interconnection, of feedback, of democracy and consensus. What we do effects what we are, what we feel, what we are becoming and pervades our experience and relationships. The practice of a moral ecology inclines means to ends. What we do affects us. This is the ancient law of karma, of action and effect.

If progress, if building a tower to heaven collapsed along with the imperatives of industrial civilization as a consequences of the Age of Pollution, what arose was an ecological philosophy and theology that embraced the concept of exile and return. Industrialism was an exile, ultimately a further banishment from the Garden, writ large, that threatened humanity and all creation not just with hardship, pain, and toil but extinction, the final night, the Nietschzean death, not only of G-d but of humanity and much of what lives in accompaniment to our agonies.

Industrialism was exile—ecological civilization the return. This is not the reentry into a protected paradise but the opportunity and necessity to continue the practice of healing the wounds of industrialism and maintaining the dynamic balance that allows the continuing existence of an ecological society. It is an expression of an opportunity for choice and ongoing human agency. In a sustainable world each tomorrow is decidedly a new day. But we have also been here before.

The ideas of exile and return, of human agency and responsibility drew on the insights of such people as twentieth-century German Jewish thinker and theologian Alexander Altman. Altman's life and thought was shaped in response to the rise and depredations of Hitler and Nazism. Out of this hellish cauldron, the worst that the bloody, bloody twentieth century had to offer, was a profound focus on the meaning of Jewish and moral existence and a reawakening of spiritual practice.

The elements of the ecological world, the unity that flowers from our diversity, is shaped by all aspects of human expression. It is found in the sensitive and complex organ meditations of Cesar Franck. It resides in the ethereal landscapes of a Hyman Bloom. It arises from our new vernacular architecture that flowed from the pioneering pattern language concepts in the twentieth century. It shines forth from our literature that weighs and expresses the ways we are.

The great poem that prefigured the spirit that would reach its apotheosis in the industrial age was the *Iliad*, the founding work of the Western canon, that tale of the wrath of Achilles and its bloody consequences—the *Iliad* that Simone Weil understood as the poem of force, whose violence under the eye of Homer transforms vital living men into dead things again and again.

In contrast, it is Whitman's *Leaves of Grass* that has become the founding poetic statement of the ecological age—Whitman, whose poem "I Sing the Body Electric" celebrates the renewing sensuousness and precious vitality of life that has been embraced in our times. Whitman, American Civil War journalist and nurse, witness to the slaughter of his times, as poet sang of the glories of living and of life.

The three unities of ecological philosophy, of unity in diversity, of experience and relationship, of action and consequences may perhaps be further simplified and expressed by the mythic resonance and unity in the *S'hma*, the fundamental Jewish injunction of the Torah, "Hear, O Israel, the Lord thy G-d, the Lord is one." This oneness is pervasive and universal, an expression of the essential unity and holiness and interconnection of everything. The three unities in this regard may be taken as a sort of brief manual for action to inform the underlying glory of oneness.

What's at stake, as too many centuries of human anguish demonstrated, is not the profoundness or accuracy of our truths but their daily living application. For an ecological world, the three unities will do as a basic guide to inform our ongoing and diverse practice, enabling us to triangulate to direct and equilibrate action.

The ecological worldview is not the celebration of stasis and quiescence. It requires active and profound engagement. We need to get off our asses. Just sitting around in the Town Hall complaining doesn't cut it. What's needed is the careful expression and practice of human agency.

Humanity at the end of the Age of Pollution had to limit and transform its individual and collective conduct or face extinction—humanity, having evolved self-consciousness and developed technology that transcended, or at least conditionally suspended, the usual biological limits placed on other species.

Yes, the dinosaurs ruled the earth, that is, they lived as the dominant animals for about 100 million years. Humanity as the genus *Homo* threatened to vanish after just one million years, having risen to notable prominence for maybe one-hundred thousand years, or just a tenth of that one million. It was the ecological consequences of unprecedented human technological activity that devastated and profoundly altered biological and even geological processes that threatened to decimate or even destroy the human species.

The earth would recover from the consequences of human depredations, and the evolution of self-consciousness of surviving marine mammals would continue, offering an alternative and perhaps highly preferable expression of a waterworld high culture. But that would have been on a world without humanity.

Down by the River

Would that I could say that we are different people now, that the bold Universal Declaration of Human Rights and Sustainability has become integral to our souls and that we act instinctively and wisely in a way that, by its nature, makes a repeat of the agonies of the past not just conditionally unthinkable but actually impossible. We have not crossed that river. It remains forever unfordable. We remain, as ever, in the midst of the river, plunging downstream, as ever required to make choices about how to steer, judgments on what rapids to run and when to back off and portage.

We are not better people. But, in response to necessity, we have built a sustainable and ecological world. It hasn't been easy. We have made sacrifices and trade-offs. There have been streams we did not follow despite their allure and our desires. Sustainability has not reduced the ten thousand things to one thing. But we have put the ten thousand things in some kind of comprehensible perspective. Violence counts less. Materialism has been relegated more to the spiritual than the physical realm. In this way we have perhaps fooled ourselves. But we have also cut our losses and constrained their consequences. Is the best I can say of our Happy Days is that we have discovered ways to cut our losses?

But the constraint upon hubris is also the constraint upon tragedy. The hard, hard lessons of the ecological transformation were not only that everything is connection but that our choices have consequences and, in the end, are paramount in determining what happens and why—not necessarily in the way we supposed, but, nevertheless, as consequences indeed.

There are fewer of us, and we live longer. There are far fewer poor, and that is a joy. And there are far fewer children, and that is a sadness. But our children are well loved and well cared for, and that is fortunate indeed.

The great lesson perhaps of our success, if we can claim that for the ecological transformation, is that we have managed to exchange the pursuit of power for the experience of pleasure. In this way, our turn from the acquisitive endless material to the satisfied sustainable *enough* was a very good deal and a real bargain.

Curmudgeon and reality-monger though I am, I must admit that we have accomplished what was believed to have been impossible. We transformed a global industrial system of warring nation-states into an ecological civilization where peace, not war, is the norm, and justice and fairness is the common expression of individual and collective democratic self-interest. That's why I've written—to remind us where we've been and how we've arrived here. Where we are going is another matter.

It's often said of economists and prophets that they had forecast five out of the last two economic downturns or the end of the world often enough that when such things finally seemed about to happen they were acclaimed as seers. The way forward for us is not to retrace our steps or to make the error that has afflicted humanity so many times before us: to think that we can simply project our present course indefinitely into the future.

The basic dynamics of excess calling forth countervailing responses, and society resolving intractable problems through an increase in scale and social complexity have not been repealed. The forces that brought us here, like the forces still moving the continents across the face of this planet, are still at work.

The continental-unions, like nation-states before them are not immutable. Neither are any of the social innovations I have so proudly recounted as evidence of successful democratic derring-do. They too in time will have served their purpose and will have to change. The ecological and sustainable world of today is not the end state.

We have choices to make. Shall we have more wild lands and still fewer people, as is under Union consideration in proposals for the return of wilderness, not just its preservation? Shall we have fewer but somewhat larger cities, with more people and with a ring of satellite communities surrounded by wilderness? Will the connection between art and commerce and play in the networked world continue to evolve and deepen? Or shall we further confine commerce and exchange and increasingly withdraw from the enterprise side of life to pursue our arts and pleasures more, solely for their own sakes? Will such fragmentation into those who earn and those who do not, court unsustainable divisions and stresses? Shall we continue to actively explore life extension and flirt with the consequences of a conditional immortality and its drastic consequences?

The point is that the problems raised in finding a balance to the demands of the material and the industrial megamachine have been replaced by a new set of emerging questions raised by the dynamics of a sustainable and ecological world. Sustainability does not mean an end state or stasis. It means the possibility to continuing, not a guarantee of an agreement upon a future course of action. Sustainability has preserved our options. It has not foreclosed them. Indeed, it has opened new and more complex choices for us that are unimpeded by the overriding industrial concerns for more production, more consumption, and more power.

Instead, we have to cope with the differing imperatives of sustainability and their consequences. Turning from the material and embracing limits and the sensuous was a beginning. It was not enough, and it was not the end. It raises, for you and for your children's children to come, ever more profound, challenging, and interesting questions to resolve for yourselves and for our democracy as you define what freedom and community means in your times.

It's a glorious afternoon on the rocks bathed in the low-angled sun near the Warner River. Red-winged blackbirds are scampering and chirping in the brush. A great blue heron hunts in the shallows. A kid is casting flies into the river, hoping for a trout before the sun sets. It's time for me to close this book. What matters is that there have been days like this for generations before, and it seems likely to continue for generations to come. That's what we've worked for and have been fortunate enough to see come to pass. It's up to us and to you, the coming generations, to help it continue.

Notes

page 25 *The Writings of George Washington*, edited by John C. Fitzpatrick, 26:227.

page 84 Lewis Mumford, *The Myth of the Machine: The Pentagon of Power* (New York: Harcourt, Brace, Jovanovich, 1970), 403.

22nd-Century Aphorisms and Quotations

Utopia? What can anyone who can still tell the difference between a cowpie and a potpie say to that?

If the market rules are right, the price points the way.

A smart market means you can do well and good.

Let me just tell you one word you need to know about your future: Mustard.

Efficiency, without concern for consequences, is the handmaiden of industrialism and injustice and the enemy of democracy and sustainability.

The twenty-second century is the era of no brand.

In the cooperative world, unemployment is the last, not the first, recourse of business.

The twentieth-century sense of separation of democracy and economy no longer obtains in the twenty-second century.

Freedom and community find new expression through the pursuit of sustainability.

Sustainability is not something to be achieved and then put in a box or a rule book or codified by law. Sustainability is ever in motion, ever a matter for disputation and democratic debate and for sometimes hard choices.

The industrial model is: We act, the living world adapts.

I sit here at 96, now middle-aged, enjoying my extended prime.

For me to have sustainbably more, everyone must have enough.

Life is a trip. But life must be more than just tripping.

The defeat of the Empire of Oil, unlike the destruction of the Cotton Kingdom, did not require a bloody civil war.

It was not science or new ideas that saved us.

We tax the bads and not the goods.

Buy cheap, save the planet.

Once poison power had to charge the true costs of production and use, the Renewable Revolution began in earnest.

Business ethics is sustainable business.

Sustainability is the way to maximize present and future value.

Democracy in the end proved to be the only effective choice. Who else could solve our problems for us?

The twenty-second century will prove Ben Franklin wrong about some things, and taxes, if not death, will prove ephemeral.

The paradox of our brave new world is that by extending our life span we have also radically limited our conduct.

Gone in this century are the old intrusive bureaucracies, with the stigma of welfare or the dole, by any euphemism.

The focus became not what to buy, but what we could avoid buying.

Human freedom and community and human reason itself could only be kept so long in thrall to the machine.

Our simple life rests upon an exquisitely complex industrial ecology.

So simple, it's global.

As traditional capitalism crumbled, an ecological world rose to replace the industrial one.

In our century we have reduced, sometimes even eliminated, the distinction between work and okay and art.

Gratification need not be endlessly postponed.

Sustainability meant not only was there no need to quest for the self-destructive and meaningless *more*, it was a positive good to search for the sufficient *enough*.

Unity in diversity is the clarion call of ecology, of co-evolution.

Experience and relationship as sensuous unity is the immediate context of an ecological world.

The practice of a moral ecology is the connection of action to consequences.

Unity in diversity, experience and relationship, the practice of a moral ecology must be lived as well as thought.

Industrialism was exile—ecological civilization the return.

Is the best I can say of our Happy Days is that we have discovered ways to cut our losses? But the constraint of hubris is also the constraint of tragedy.

Sustainability has preserved our options. It has not foreclosed them.

We are not better people. But, in response to necessity, we have built a sustainable and ecological world.

What matters is that there have been glorious days like this for generations before. It's up to us, and to you, the coming generations, to help it continue.